NIGERIAN DEMOCRACY
AND
DEMOCRACTIC EXPERIENCE

AN HISTORICAL, POLITICAL, ECONOMIC, SOCIAL AND RELIGIOUS ANALYSIS

By

KAYODE ASOGA – ALLEN

(REVISED EDITION)

First Published 2009

ISBN 1533523886

www.kayodeasogaallen.com

DEDICATION

This book is dedicated to His Excellency late Gani Fawehinmi, a legal luminary, a Senior Advocate of Nigeria (SAN), a Senior Advocate of the Masses (SAM), an epitome of a just, ideal and egalitarian society, a human rights activitist and a true and authentic elder statesman who never compromised with corrupt and self-centred individuals. It is true that Gani Fawehinmi has left Nigeria with her problems, however the people he left behind would continue to champion his noble course until Nigerian masses are liberated from the bondage of poverty, slavery, hunger, diseases and penury which just below one percent (1%) of the population of Nigeria has subjected them to.

The journey may be tedious and hazardous, many innocent lives may be wasted, but at the end it would become history. Nigeria would become a place to be. Nigerians would no longer be a nuisance and a nonentity in foreign land, seeking greener pasture. Everyone would be proud to be a Nigerian and there would be equal opportunity for everyone.

PREFACE

Nigeria obtained her political independence over five decades ago but there seems not to be much development or progress to show for it. Nigeria is like stagnant water that flows nowhere or a baby of five years that only crawls and cannot walk. The abundant resources the nation is endowed with has been cornered and are being cornered by less than one percent (1%) of Nigerians while the Nigerian masses wallow in the ocean of poverty and penury.

Those who rule the nation seem to owe the governed no obligation. This is because voting does not determine winners in Nigerian electioneering process. Winners were already made before the election date. The masses in most cases were not allowed to pick a candidate of their choice, the powerful, wealthy and corruptly minded individuals constitute themselves to a "Kabal" perform the role of king makers, and pick among themselves and force their nominated candidates on the masses. Whoever is nominated and enthroned, do the will of the "Kabal" not of the masses.

The executive nominate or appoint service chiefs in the Army, Navy and Airforce. Also he appoints the Inspector General of Police, the Chairman Electoral Commission and the same President is a contestant in the election to be handled by the Chairman Electoral Commission. This is not only ridiculous but portrays Nigeria as a country where fraudulent activities are legitimized. When you call the Electoral Commission appointed by the president "Independent", who is fooling who? No appointee would like to do something against the interest of someone who appointed him.

With all the resources of the nation, the Nigerian masses are suffering. The role of government is not felt anywhere, for example, every Nigerian today is the provider of his security and social amenities like electricity, water and so on. Government is now about those who hold political appointments not about the masses. Nigerian roads are death traps, education is poorly funded, the nation now witnesses incessant teachers' strike, and government is not bothered because public schools in Nigeria are for the poor masses. Children of those in government are in expensive private schools at home and abroad. Politicians use education as an instrument for winning election, but after winning election, they turn against it.

According to 2009 rating of the World Bank, Nigerian politicians are the highest paid politicians in the world and Nigerian workers are said to be the least paid workers in the world. This rating is true to a large extent because the resources of the nation is shared by the politicians, that is the reason there is little or nothing remaining to construct roads, provide electricity and fund education. Year in year out the situation of Nigeria is getting worse, This situation informs the concern of the author to write this book. The author is greatly worried about the future of Nigeria and Nigerians as the present crop of politicians seem to have no plan for the nation and her people but for themselves and their immediate families.

The book no doubt would enrich the readers knowledge about the situation of Nigeria right from independence till date, the level of maturity displayed by Nigerian politicians, why Nigerians are in the midst of plenty and are starving, the type of democracy Nigeria is practising and the role played by some past and present leaders to impoverish the nation.

I am highly appreciative of those who have contributed directly or indirectly to the successful completion of this book, particularly the various authors, writers, pamphleteers, newspapers, magazines to mention a few as already indicated in the reference section of this book. I wish to specifically thank the Provost of Michael Otedola College of Primary Education, Professor Oguntoye A. O. for creating a peaceful atmosphere for academic works in the College as a result of his love for peace and insistence that peaceful atmosphere is a pre-requisite for academic excellence. I must also thank the former Provost of the College, Professor Tunde Samuel for the great role he played in inculcating the culture of writing and research in the academic staff of the College during his tenure. Also I wish to thank Mr. Ogunniyi, J. O. and Dr. (Mrs.) Ojetunde C. F. for assisting in going through the manuscripts and making the necessary corrections.

Lastly, I wish to thank all my colleagues (both senior and

junior) at Michael Otedola College of Primary Education, (MOCPED) and all members of my family. They have all contributed to the success of this book.

Kayode Asoga-Allen
B.A. Ed. (History) Ogun.
M.Ed,
PhD in view

Table of Contents

CHAPTER ONE: GEOGRAPHICAL LOCATION OF NIGERIA

Introduction

Nigeria as an African country is located in the west coast of Africa. It has as its neighbours, the Republic of Niger and Chad in the north, the Republic of Cameroun in the east and the Republic of Benin in the West. The Atlantic Ocean is the Southern boundary of Nigeria. Nigeria is a large country extended over a vast land. The country occupies a land mass of 98 million hectares in which 75% represents five ecological zones suitable for agriculture including arable farming, forestry, livestock and fisheries (Ekemode, Arabambi and Sanbe, 2000). Nigeria has a territory covering about 725,000 sq kms and according to census (2006), a population of about 140 million. From north to south, it is approximately 1,300kms and about 1,100 kms east to west.

Nigeria is made up of 36 states with Abuja as the Federal Capital Territory. These states are Abia, Adamawa, , Akwa Ibom, Anambra, Bauchi, Benue, Bornu, Cross River, Delta, Edo, Enugu, Imo, Jigawa, Kaduna, Katsina, Kano, Kebbi, Kogi, Kwara, Lagos, Niger, Ogun, Ondo, Osun, Oyo, Plateau, Rivers, Sokoto, Taraba, Yobe, Ekiti, Ebonyi, Bayelsa, Nasarawa and Zamfara.

Vegetation and Climate

Nigeria has three major types of vegetation namely: rain

forest, Savannah, grassland and Sahel (Semi-desert). Nigeria has a tropical climate with two main seasons. These include the rainy season and the dry season. The rainy season starts in April and lasts till August and the dry season starts from September to March. However, in some parts of the coastal area, rain begins earlier than April and continues into October and beyond.

Crops and Minerals

Nigeria is well known in Africa and even in the whole world to be a producer of the following products, they are cotton, groundnut, cocoa, banana, maize, guinea corn, millet, cassava, plantain, rice, beans, yams, rubber, palm oil, palm kernel, tomatoes, sweet potatoes to mention a few. Apart from these agricultural produce hitherto mentioned, the following minerals are found in Nigeria in large quantity. They are crude oil, coal, bitumen, tin, marble, limestone and so on and so forth. Nigeria is blessed with fertile land that is good for agriculture and about 65 percent of Nigerian population may be said to be engaging in farming. Though the most rampant system of farming are subsistence farming that is done by a farmer and usually members of his family. The target is to feed self with little or nothing to sell. The reason for small scale nature of such farm is the fact that agriculture in the country is still being done with crude implements. Agriculture has not been mechanized due to the absence of indigenous technology and the expensive nature of acquiring and maintaining foreign or transferred technology.

The History and People of Nigeria

Virtually all the native races of Africa are represented in Nigeria, hence the great diversity of her people and culture. It was in Nigeria that the Bantu migrating from Southern and Central Africa intermingled with Sudanese. Later on other groups, such as Shuwa Arabs, the Tuaregs and the Fulanis, who are concentrated in the far north, entered northern Nigeria in migratory waves across Sahara Desert. The earliest occupants of Nigeria settled in the forest belt and in the Niger-Delta region. Today, they are estimated to be more than 250 ethnic groups in Nigeria. While no single group enjoys an absolute numeric majority, four major groups constitute about 60 percent of the population, Hausa-Fulani in the north, Yoruba in the west and Igbo in the east. Other groups include: Kanuri, Binis, Ibiobio, Ijaw, Itsekiri, Efik, Nupe and Jukun.

Empires

Kanem-Borno: While there is no direct evidence to link the people of the Jos Plateau with the Nok culture, or the Eze Nri of today with Igbo Ukwu, the history of Bornu date back to the 19th century when Arabic writers in the North Africa first noted the kingdom of Kanem East of Lake Chad. Bolstered by trade with the Nile region and Trans-Saharan trade routes, the empire prospered. In the next centuries, complex political and social systems were developed, particularly after the Bulala invasion in the 14th century. The empire moved from Kanem Borno, hence the name. The empire lasted for 1,000 years (until 19th century) despite challenges from the Hausas Fulani in the West and Jukum from the South.

Hausa-Fulani: To the west of Borno around 1,000 AD the Hausa were building similar states around Kano, Zaria, Daura, Katsina and Gobir. However, unlike the Kanuri, no ruler among these states ever became powerful enough to impose his will over the others. Although, the Hausa had common languages, culture and Islamic religion, they had no common king. Kano, the most powerful of these states controlled much of the Hausa land in the 16th and 17th centuries but conflicts with surrounding states ended this dominance. Because of these conflicts, the Fulanis, led by Usman Dan Fodio in 1804, successfully challenged the Hausa states and set up the Hausa-Fulani Caliphate with headquarters in Sokoto, commanding a broad area from Katsina in the far north to Ilorin, across the River Niger.

Yoruba: In the West, the Yoruba developed complex powerful city states. The first of these important states were Ile-Ife, which according to Yoruba mythology was centre of the universe. Ife is the site of a unique art form first uncovered in the 1930s. Naturalistic terracotta, bronze-heads and other artefacts dealing as far back as the 10th century show just how early the Yoruba developed an advanced civilization. Later, other Yoruba cities challenged Ife for supremacy and Oyo became the most powerful West African kingdom in the 16th and 17th centuries. The armies of Oyo king (Alaafin) dominated other Yoruba cities and even forced tributes from the ruler of Dahomey. Internal struggle and the Fulani expansion to the south caused the collapse of the Oyo in the early 19th century.

Benin: Benin developed into a major kingdom during the same period that Oyo was becoming dominant in the west. Although, the people of Benin are primarily Edo not Yoruba they share with Ife and Oyo many of the origins and there is much evidence of cultural and artistic interchange between the kingdoms. The king (Oba) of Benin was considered semi-divine and controlled a complex bureaucracy, a large army and a diversified economy. Benin power reached the apex in the 16th century.

Igbo and the Delta States: Many Nigerian cultures did not develop into centralised monarchies. Of these, the Igbo are probably the most remarkable because of the size of their territory and the density of population. Igbo societies were organised in self-contained villages or federations of village communities, with a society of elders and age-grade associations sharing various governmental functions. The same way was true of the Ijaw of the Niger-Delta and people of the Cross River area, where secret societies also played a prominent role in administration and governmental functions. But by the 18th century overseas trade had began to encourage the emergence of centralized systems of government.

South West Nigeria

Abeokuta means "under the rock" derived from the Olumo Rock, the town's most famous landmark. Abeokuta the capital of Ogun State, lies on the Ogun River and rugged, rocky hills, offering excellent photo opportunities. Home of Adire cloth; Abeokuta has an intriguing array of markets which sell a wide range of exotic goods. Olumo rock sacred to the Egba people, is on the east side of the Ogun River. Visitors should engage a guide from the tourist centre at the bottom of the rock where one can explore the caves used as sanctuary during the Yoruba civil war. At the rock summit, visitors can enjoy a tremendous view of Abeokuta and the Ogun River.

Benin City: Benin City is stepped in history. World renowned Benin bronze sculptures date back to the 15th century when the Oba of Benin ruled the large and powerful Edo kingdom, a period when bronze casting was an art used to glorify the Oba. In 1897, a British Expeditionary Force sacked Benin and took many of the Bronze to London, still several good examples of the bronze artefacts remain in both Benin and Lagos Museums. Today, Bronze casting still continues in several streets in the city, including Igun and Oloton streets. Another attraction in Benin is Chief Ogiamen's house, a prime example of Benin traditional architecture built before 1897. The house miraculously survived the "Great fire" which destroyed a significant part of the city during that period.

Ibadan: Ibadan is one of the largest indigenous African cities. Located along the edge of a thickly wooded forest belt, it was called Eba-Odan, meaning at the edge of the forest. Today, it is the capital and main commercial centre of Oyo State. Places of interest in Ibadan include Dugbe market, a huge traditional market place, the Parliament Building, the University of Ibadan-Nigeria's Premier University, its Teaching Hospital and Cocoa House. The first Television Station in Nigeria was established in Ibadan by Chief Obafemi Awolowo. Ibadan is also close to the historic towns of Oyo, Ogbomosho, Ijebu-Ode, Ife, Ilesha and Oshogbo

Ile Ife: The ancient city of Ile-Ife, in Osun State, is truly unique. The Yorubas consider it to be the cradle of creation and civilization. Legend says it was at Ife that Oduduwa sent by Olodumare, the Yoruba god of creation, established the first land upon the waters that covered the earth, thus founding Ife. It is soon spread to other parts of Yoruba to create further kingdoms. Ile-Ife became a remarkable centre for arts, producing both terracotta figures and bronzes dating from 12th to 15th centuries, second in fame only to the Benin bronzes.

Lagos: It was a trading post between the Benin kingdom and the Portugeues until the arrival of British traders in the 19th century, presaging the colonization of the interior. Lagos is divided into several parts, each with its distinctive character. The heart of the city is Lagos Island (Eko) containing most of

Nigeria's commercial and administrative headquarters. It is linked to the mainland by three road bridges and to Ikoyi Island and Victoria Island by road. The latter are mostly residential areas with palatial houses, expensive gardens and five star hotels in a gorgeous setting. Tourist attractions in the city include the National Museum, the National Theatre and miles of beautiful beaches. Oba's palace sits majestically on Lagos Island, portions of which are over 200 years old with a newly constructed extension.

Ondo: Ondo has many fascinating tourist attractions including the Ikogosi warm spring, Idanre Hills, Ipolo-Iloro waterfalls, Ebomi Lake and the Museum at Owo. The most popular are Ikogosi Warm Spring and the Idanre Hills. The Ikogosi Warm Spring located in a valley in Ikogosi town, north-east of Akure, is ideal for camping or picnics. The Idanre hills with curious dome-shaped peaks are located in Idanre, southwest of Akure. The hills have socio-religious significance, having protected inhabitants from invaders during inter-ethnic wars in the historic past.

Southeast Nigeria

Anambra State: Anambra state offers many exciting attractions throughout the area. These include the Ogunike caves, Agulu Lake, Igbo-Ukwu archaeological excavations and the Aguleri Games Reserve. Onitsha, located on the Eastern bank of the River Niger, is famous for its robust market and commercial activity. The traditional ofala festivals, performed by royally in Anambra are rare pageants of colour and fanfare.

Calabar is an attractive city on the bank of the new Calabar River, near its confluence with the Cross River, which has a long history as the regional port of eastern Nigeria. Residents here trace their ancestors back to Babylon before the time of Christ.

First visited by the Portuguese at the end of the 15th century, Calabar is also the centre from which many missionaries ventured forth in the 19th and 20th centuries, including Mary Slessor who arrived in Calabar in 1875. Places of interest include the National Museum in the old Residency Building. The building was prefabricated, shipped from Britain and erected on top Consular Hill which was later known as Government Hill in 1884. The Museum itself is history. The Museum traces the history of Calabar and the surrounding areas in a spacious setting.

Enugu is the centre of the Nigerian coal industry. Situated in attractive hilly country with wide roads, expressways and main arteries leading to the North, South, East and West. Sites in Enugu include a branch of the National Museum, the Iva Valley Coal Mine Museum (where coal was first mined in 1909), and University of Nigeria Faculties. It can also boast of one of the best hotels in Nigeria, the Nike Lake Hotel.

Oron is in the south-east corner of the Akwa Ibom state, on the Cross River, and is worth visiting for its National Museum. The Museum overlooking the river encases the history of the local Ibibo people plus an important collection of wooden Ekpo memorial carvings that portray the male ancestors of the Ibibo people, believed to be two to three centuries old.

Owerri is predominantly inhabited by the Igbo people. The Igbos are renowned for their music and dancing, especially the colourful masquerades in which the dancer wear elaborate masks. Places of interest include an amusement park, the Nekedu Botanical and Zoological Gardens, the Palm Beach Tourist Village at Awomama and the Oguta Lake Holiday Resort, which has developed into an International Tourist Centre.

Portharcourt is the capital of Rivers State and is the centre of the oil industry in Nigeria. It is called the "Garden City" because of its abundance of trees and parks. It is now the second most important port in Nigeria. Port Harcourt did not exist before 1913. Nearby are two historic Ports of Bonny and Brass formerly connected with the slave trade, but which now serve as oil ports and terminals. The town is a good base from which to explore the local creek villages and towns. The local people include Efik, Kalabari, Ogoni and Ibos, not to mention British, French, American and Dutch, who work in the oil fields. Sites include the State Museum, which features many examples of local culture including masks and carvings. The cultural centre of Bonny Street has a stage and auditorium for plays, dancing and a shop where tourists can purchase local handicrafts. The Azumint Blue River Sports, beautiful clear water with sandy beaches. Tourists can rent canoes for a ride down the river to stop at a beach side picnic site, outfitted with wooden chairs, tables and grills for a pleasant ride barbecue

Umuahia is home to the National War Museum where relics of the Nigerian civil war are on display, including weapons and fascinating local inventions. Other inventions include the Akwette Blue River Tourist Village and Uwana Beach. Visitors to Akwette will be impressed with its unique weaving industry.

Central Nigeria

Abuja in 1976, was selected by the Federal Government to become the new seat of government and in 1992, the first four stages of this movement to Abuja was launched with the most of the senior government officials now in Abuja. Besides being the administrative seat of government, Abuja is a beautiful city surrounded by rolling hills, with ample mountaineering potential. The Gwagwa Hills, near Suleja, the Chukuku Hills, the Agwa Hills and the famous Zuma rocks are just some of the awe inspiring manifestations of nature's beauty in the area.

Bida is a lively town, famous for its handicrafts and colourful market and is the principal cityof the Nupe people. Bida is famous for its glass beads, cloths, silver and brass work, its carved 8-legged stools made from a single piece of wood and decorative pottery. Bida's market truly stands out as a traditional show case of local commerce in Nigeria

Gurara Falls is on the Gurara River in Niger State, on the road between Suleja and Minna. Particularly impressive during the rainy season, the falls span 200 metres across with a sheer drop of 30 meters, which creates a dazzling rainbow effects as the water cascades over the top into a cloud of spray below.

Ilorin: an ancient city, is the southernmost point of fulani expansion and bears characteristics of both North and South. It has often been described as the gateway between the two because of its strategic location, and as a result offers a good base for visiting the surrounding area. Tourist sites in Ilorin include the Mimi's Mosque and residence built during the reign of Zul-Gambari, the late Emir of Ilorin. Both attest to the Islamic Culture of the city. Another attraction is the Dada pottery workshop in Okelele quarters. It is the largest pottery factory in Nigeria. Other local tourist sites in Kwara State include the Essie Museum Stone figures. Over 1,000 soap stone figures of men and women, sitting on stools or kneeling, with elaborate hair styles and facial marks. Little is known about the figures, being products of a very old civilization. Esie Museum houses the largest collection of stone figures in sub-saharan Africa.

Owu Fall: In Kwara State is the highest and most spectacular natural water fall in West Africa, at its best during the rainy season. The water fall cascade 330 feet down an escapement with rocky outcrops to a pool of ice-cold water below.

Lokoja: It is a historic town. Due to its location at the confluence of the two great rivers, the Niger and Benue, it became the headquarters of the Royal Niger Company in the 19th century. The headquarters building, still standing, was prefabricated in London and shipped to Nigeria, where it was assembled without using a single nail. Also in Lokoja is the Iron of Liberty, located in the compound of the first primary school in northern Nigeria. Here, many slaves were freed at the end of the slave trade.

Makurdi: It is located on the bank of River Benue, one of the two great rivers in Nigeria. For visitors to the area, there is a zoological garden in Makurdi and Goven Hills, Ushango Hills and Bassa Hills including fishing and boating on the Benue River, in Igbor there is the Ikure Wildlife Park.

Okene: It is the home of the Igbira, an industrious people renowned for their farming abilities and their beautiful woven cloth, picturesque Okene, nestled atop several rocky hills, is a fascinating place to visit. The craft of the cloth weaving still continues to thrive here and the cloth remains highly prized throughout Nigeria, for tourists in the area, Okene has a thriving market, open every other day, where there is a section dedicated for the woven cloth.

Koton-Karfi: It is located west of Okene and about 20 miles north of the confluence of the rivers Niger and Benue. For anyone who enjoys fishing, Koton-Karfi is a paradise, for the multiples of Niger tributaries and teeming with fish.

NorthEast Nigeria

Bauchi: This is an old Hausa town surrounded by an appealing range of rolling hills. It is close to both the Yankari Game Reserve, approximately $1^1/_2$ hours away from the southeast and the site of Geji Rock Painting located on the Bauchi Jos Road. In Bauchi, tourists may also visit a memorial and library dedicated to Sir Abubakar Tafawa Balewa, the first Prime Minister of Nigeria, who was assassinated in 1966. The Library houses many of Balewa's personal papers.

Jos: It has always been a popular destination for tourists due to its height above sea level (4062 feet). Jos has two golf courses, Ray field and Plateau, plus a polo club and other sports/entertainment offerings. The National Museum in Jos is one of the best in Nigeria especially for archaeology and pottery, where many fine examples of Nok heads and artefacts, circa 500BC - 200AD, are displayed. The Pottery Hall has an exceptional collection of finely crafted pottery from all over the country. On the same grounds, the museum of architecture contains life-size replicas of Nigeria architecture, from the walls of Kano to the mosque of Zaria to a Tiv village. Other attractions in the area include the wildlife park, nestled amidst 8sqkm (3.09sq miles) of unspoiled savannah bush where the rare pigmy hippopotamus is successfully being bred 'hippo pool'.

Lions roam a large enclosure that simulates their natural habitat and visitors will also find elephants, red river hogs, jackals, chimpanzees, crocodiles and numerous other animals to view. The Shere Hills can be seen to the east of Jos and offer a prime view of the city below. Assop falls is a small water fall (again best seen in rainy season) which could make a pleasant picnic spot on a drive from Jos to Abuja. Riyon Rock is a dramatic and photogenic pile of rocks balanced precariously on top of one another, with one resembling a clown's hat, observable from the main Jos-Gimi Road. Kura falls is a refreshing area for walks and picnics, with scenery reminiscent of the Scottish highlands.

Maiduguri: It is a handsome, impressive town with broad streets and plentiful trees, presiding over strong traditions and a culture dating back more than 1,000 years. Maiduguri is an ideal place for seeing the Kanuri people, with their fine tribal markings, and the Shuwa women, adorned with plaited hairstyles and flowing gowns.

The Borno Region: Around Maiduguri is one of the most fascinating places in Nigeria. Along the northern borders of the state is Sahel-Savannah country, endowed with rolling sand dunes punctuated by oases in the dry season, yet covered with vegetation during the rainy season. Southern Borno is generally green savannah land, enlivened by hills and rock formations. While towards the Cameroun border, visitors will enjoy majestic mountain visages.

The Bulatori Oases: These are on the western side of Borno State northeast of Nguru. This is the desert in a Hollywood film set: dunes, camels and palm tree around an oasis. The severe beauty of this place offers a special treat to visitors who are yet to experience such daunting landscape. The oases are also excellent for bird watchers: in the dry season there are thousands of Palaearctic migrants which congregate there.

Yola: It is located at the upper reaches of the Benue River, lies in close proximity to some of the most scenic areas of Nigeria, situated along the mountainous border with Cameroun. The Mambilla Plateau is within a day journey from Yola, as are the Sebshi Mountains in the south.

The Gwoza Hills: These are breath taking. They are located southeast of Maiduguri, and southeast of the village of Gwoza valley, along the Cameroun border.

Mandara Mountain: These are also in the area stretching from south, in Mambilla, to Mubi in the north. The Mandaras provide some of the most spectacular scenery in all of Africa, it is suggested that tourists in the area take at least a week to enjoy both the Nigeria and Cameroun sides of these mountains.

Northwest Nigeria

Kano City: It is the oldest major city in sub-sahara Africa, dates back more than thousand years. For centuries, it was one of the most active commercial centres in West Africa. Today, it is the Nigeria's third largest city in the North. Centrally located Kano city acts as a terminus for the whole of northern Nigeria. It is linked by road and communications with all other major population centres in the region. By virtue of its historic role as trading centre between the Sahara, down south to Zaria, Kano remains a living, modern day relic of a rich past.

The Emir's palace in Kano is the past incarnate with its old stone walls and entrance gate at the heart of the ancient city, encircled by a wall that extended to 11.7km in circumference, with sixteen different gates. Closed by, the Gidan Makama Museum offers an excellent history of Kano and of the Hausa and Fulani peoples. Kano Central Mosque is one of the largest in Nigeria and, with permission; a visitor may be allowed to ascend one of its towering mine rates to gain a spectacular view of the city.

Kaduna: It was previously the colonial capital of Northern Nigeria. Located on the Kaduna River, the city serves as an important junction, with road extending in five different directions. Kaduna is a major communication centre and industrial base but also a thriving metropolis from which tourists can explore the surrounding country side. Within Kaduna, there is a National Museum on Ali Akilu Road that features wood carvings, masks, Nok, terracotta figures and Benin bronzes. Plans are underway to have an annual Durbar festival in Kaduna like the 1977 Durbar festival that drew all the northern Emirs to Kaduna

Katsina: This is the northernmost city in Nigeria, sits on the edge of Sahel and borders the neighbouring country of Niger, which has traded with her for centuries. Katsina, one of the walled Hausa cities is the capital of Katsina State. The

Goborau market, a most picturesque tourist attraction is the tallest mud-brick building in Nigeria and is 250 years old. A fine view of Katsina can be gained from the top, in area that host the best and the most elaborate Durbar festivals

Birnin Kebbi: It is a century old Hausa-Fulani walled city, it is the capital of the newly created Kebbi State. The area is famous for traditional arts and crafts, beads, sword and glassware, and is the site of the Argungu fishing festival, one of the most popular tourist attractions in Nigeria. Held annually, it attracts competitors from neighbouring Niger and Chad Republics, plus many visitors from all over the world. Apart from the traditional fishing competition, there are also boxing and wrestling contests.

Sokoto: It is the centre of Islamic activities in Nigera, the home of Sultan of Sokoto, the spiritual leader of Muslims in the country. The city stretches with avenues of lush trees and wide roads appearing like an oasis in a semi-desert area. Sokoto is another of the great trading cities of the north. It is linked with trade routes across the Sahara to Morocco and Algeria. It is famous for its excellent leather work: handbags, wallets, fans and other items featuring exquisite crafting. The Sultan palace is a delightful sight, with its lavish architectural and guards in their multi-colour regalia. At 9.00p.m. On Thursdays, visitors can watch the musicians play Tambari for the Sultan. Usman Dan Fodio, the founder of the present day Hausa-Fulani states, is buried in Sokoto. Though, not a tourist site per se, it holds great historical importance

Zaria: It is one of the original seven Hausa cities founded in the 16th century, it is a vibrant attractive city which has retained its ancient look by leaving most of the modern development and industry to nearby Kaduna. Once surrounded by some 19km of walls, in some areas, still well preserved, Zaria has three important establishments: The Ahmadu Bello University at Samaru Quarters, the first university in the north, Barewa College, the oldest high school in the north, where most of the Nigerian political and military leaders were educated and finally, the Nigerian School of Civil Aviation, the only one of its kind in West Africa.

CHAPTER TWO: THE ORIGIN OF GOVERNMENT

Introduction

Man born in a family, is compelled to maintain a society, from necessity, from natural inclination and from habit. The same creature, in his further progress, is engaged in establishing political society, in order to administer justice; without which there can be no peace, or safety, or mutual relationship among members of the political entity. We are therefore, to look upon all the vast apparatus of our government, as having ultimately no other object or purpose than that of distribution of justice, or in other words, the support of the twelve judges, kings and parliaments, fleet of armies, officers of the court and revenue, ambassadors, ministers and privy-counsellors, who are all subordinate in their end to this important part of political administration. Even the clergy, as their duty leads them to inculcating morality, may justly be thought, as regards this world to have no other useful object of their institution except justice.

All men are sensible of the necessity of justice for the purpose of maintaining peace and order, and all men are sensible of the necessity of peace and order for the maintenance of just and egalitarian society. Notwithstanding this strong and obvious necessity, such is the fragility or perverseness of our nature! It is impossible to keep men faithfully and unerringly, in paths of justice. Some extra-ordinary circumstances may happen in which a man finds his interest to be more promoted by fraud or rapine, than hurt by the breach which injustice makes in the social union. But much more frequently, he is seduced from his great and important, but distant interests, by the allurement of present, though often very frivolous temptations.

Men must therefore, endeavour to palliate what they cannot cure. They must institute some persons, under the appellation of magistrates whose peculiar office it is, to point out the decrees of equity, to punish transgressors, to correct fraud and violence, and to oblige men, however reluctant, to consult their own real and permanent interests. In a word, OBEDIENCE is a new duty which must be invented to support that of JUSTICE: and the ties of equity must be corroborated by those of allegiance.

But, still viewing matters in an abstract light, it may be thought, that nothing is gained by this alliance and that the fact that duty of obedience, from its very nature, lays as feeble a hold of the human mind, as the primitive and natural duty of justice. Peculiar interest and present temptations may overcome one as well as the other. They are equally exposed to the same inconvenience. And the man, who is inclined to be a bad neighbour, must be led by the same motives, well or ill understood, to be a bad citizen and subject. Not to mention that the magistrate himself may often be negligent or partial or unjust in his administration.

Experience, however, proves that there is great difference between the cases. Order in society, we find, is much better maintained by means of government and our duty to the magistrate is more strictly guarded by the principles of human nature, than our duty to our fellow citizens. The love of dominion is so strong in the breast of man, than many, not only, submit to, but cut all the dangers, and fatigues, and cares of government: and men once raised to that station, though often led astray by private passions, find, in ordinary cases, a visible interest in the impartial administration of justice. The persons who first attain this distinction by the consent, tacit or express, of the people must be endowed with superior personal qualities of valour, force, integrity or prudence, which command respect and confidence, and after government is established, a regard to birth, rank and station has a mighty influence over men, and enforces the decrees of the magistrate. The prince or leader exclaims against every disorder which disturbs his society.

Some writers have so confounded society with government in that they live little or no distinction between them. Whereas, they are not only different, but have different origins. Society is produced by our wants, and government by our wickedness; the former promotes our happiness positively by uniting our affections, the latter negatively, by restraining our vices. One encourages intercourse, while the other creates distinctions. The former is a patron while the latter is a punisher.

Society in every state is a blessing, but Government, even in its best state, is but a necessary evil: in its worst state an intolerable one. Our calamity is heightened by reflecting that we furnish the means by which we suffer Government, like dress, is the badge of lost innocence; the palaces of kings are built upon the ruins of the bowers of paradise. For where the impulses of conscience are clear; uniform and irresistibly obeyed, man would need no other law giver. But that is not being the case. He finds it necessary to surrender up a part of his property to furnish means for the protection of the rest and this; he is induced to do by the same prudence which in every other case advises him, out of two evils to choose the least. Wherefore, security, being the true design and end of government, it unanswerably follows that whatever form thereof appears most likely to ensure it to us, with the least expense and greatest benefit, is preferable to all others.

In order to gain a clear and just idea of the design and end of government, let us suppose a small number of persons settled in some sequester part of the earth unconnected with the rest; they will then represent the first peopling of any country, or of the world. In this state of natural liberty, society will be their first thought. A thousand motives will excite them thereto; the strength of one man is so unequal to his wants, and his mind so unfitted for perpetual solitude, that he is soon obliged to seek assistance and relief of another who in his turn requires the same. Four or five united would be able to raise a tolerable dwelling in the midst of a wilderness, but one man might labour out the common period of life without accomplishing anything. When he had felled his timber, he could not remove it, nor erect it after it was removed. Hunger in the main time would urge him to quit his work and every different want would call him a different way. Disease, may even misfortune, would be death. For though, neither might be mortal, yet either would disable him from living and reduces him to a state in which he might rather be said to perish than to die.

The Concept of Government

Government can be defined as machinery put in place by people of a nation for the multi-dimensional purpose of administering, coordinating, regulating and overseeing their affairs. Living together has many advantages. In order to live happily, everybody needs numerous things. These needs include food, comfortable shelter, clothing, security, good education, quick and safe means of transportation, good health, refreshing entertainment, peaceful environment and tranquillity. It is very difficult for a single person to provide all these things for his own use alone. He will end up becoming a jack of all trade and master of none. In an attempt to provide all these things by a single individual, his life span may be cut short and he may die of hard labour.

When we live together, we help one another. Each person specialises in one or two things. Individual learns the work he is most interested in. He also enjoys doing it. He produces more than he personally needs and offers the surplus to the other people in the community who also specialise in other areas of his needs. Other members of the community who have specialised in various other occupations satisfy his other needs and wants. Looking at every society, you find the following people, farmer who supplies the food need of the community, teacher who sees to the education of the children, policemen who maintain law and order, soldiers who defend the territorial integrity of the state, traders who see to the distribution of the products in the community and several other people who specialise in important areas of the societal needs.

One of the advantages of living together is that it makes specialisation and cooperation possible. We help one another and thereby help ourselves. Living together in the community however, is not without some problems. First, the things like food, clothing, shelter, means of creation, money and wealth, and all the other things which help to make life happy and comfortable are always in short supply. Everyone desires then but only very little are available for a small proportion of the population.

Everybody struggles to work very hard to secure them. Since the supply is always short in proportion to the demand, competition for them sets in. It is compared to a race in which we all engage. One basic thing is that every game has rules and regulations and a referee or umpire who will see that the rules and regulations are enforced.

Indeed, if there are no rules and regulations guiding a particular game, there is likelihood for competitors to quarrel, fight, argue and cause crises. Likewise if there are rules and regulations without referee to direct and regulate the game, in order to avoid crises, chaos and fighting the rules and regulation would not achieve its goal. When we are together, we must choose a person or a group of persons whose duty is to make good regulations and laws for the people who live together and also to see the enforcement of the rules and regulations by punishing the offenders and reforming them. This person or group of persons which we choose and give mandate to make and enforce the rules, regulations and laws is referred to as the Government.

Government in Nigeria before the Advent of British Colonialists

Before the advent of the British colonialists, the geographical area known as Nigeria today were under various traditional rulers. That is to say that each ethnic group in Nigeria had organised itself into a governmental unit. Each ethnic group had a way by which it governed its people. The Yorubas, Hausas, Igbos were ruled by traditional institutions. The traditional rulers were seen as semi-god by their subjects especially among Yorubas and Hausas. It was the belief of the people that the traditional rulers had divine authority. In Yoruba land, whatever the king said was final in those days. No one dare questions the king. That manifests in the names given to the king till today. For example, in Yoruba land, the kings are called "KABIYESI" which means nobody can question him. "Alase Igbakeji Orisa", that means the Divine Authority and next to god.

The Oba was the supreme authority over the people. His decision or verdict over any issue was final. He was the Alpha and Omega. He was the greatest judge of the land, he could do and undo. To ensure effective and efficient administration of the people, the king ordained some people as chiefs. Ideally, there is a chief from each lineage. These chiefs were responsible for settling minor disputes at the local level, they were also responsible for enforcing the authority of the king among their people.

In the northern part of Nigeria, the Sarkis were in charge, the functions they perform were similar to those of the kings in the south west. Indeed, they were kings. They were highly respected and dignified. Below the sarkis were the title holders who assisted him in his administration. The sarki and his chiefs met from time to time to discuss issues affecting the people settle major disputes and made laws to guide the behaviour of the people.

In Igbo land, the situation was a bit different. The Obis or Eze who were the traditional heads of the communities did not have much authority over their subjects. Unlike the situation in Yoruba land and Hausa land where the Obas and Sarkis were seen as semi-gods and absolute authorities, in Igbo land, the Obi/Eze's authority might be rejected if people did not like it. This is because the Igbos were not organised under the kingship from their origin. There was no central government. Igbos lived in segmentary communities.

In Yoruba land and Hausa land, the traditional authorities had rights to collect tributes from their subjects. It is a basic fact that no administration can stand without finance. The tributes collected by the kings/sarkis were in cash and kind. This helped to maintain the Royal household and to strengthen the hegemony of the kings.

Feudalism was practised in the northern emirates and western Yoruba land. Though, there were some degree of difference between the way it was practised in these two ethnic regions a little difference could be observed. In the northern emirate all the subjects remained tenants on the land and they were made to pay fief or tributes to the sarki, but in Yoruba land, only strangers who came to settle in the territory and those whose towns and villages were conquered during war and annexed paid tribute as tenants to the king.

Every community had its standing soldiers who fought and defended the territory of the community. It must be stressed that not in all communities were the king's power unlimited. In some communities, there were organs of government which acted as checks and balances to the power of the obas. A typical example was the old Oyo Empire. There was an organ of government known as Oyomesi. The Oyomesis acted as checks and balances to the power of Alaafin. They ensured that the Oba was not power intoxicated, thereby becoming a tyrant. The idea of the people of old Oyo empire that put this measure in place could be likened to that of the principles of separation of power.

Power corrupts and absolute power corrupts absolutely. Thus, people ensure that the whole power of the empire were not concentrated in the hands of the Alaafin. This idea of checks and balances helped to check the excesses of the king. This became necessary as the organ had power to present a calabash to any Alaafin who proved tyranical. That is, overthrowing him by asking him to commit suicide. It is obvious that the role being performed in modern government today by legislators had been performed years ago by some traditional government in Nigeria and as such, they are not new.

The major religion of the people at that time was idol worshipping. There were gods which the communities held in high esteem. Perhaps, because of what the people claimed the gods did it one time or the other for them in the past or because they felt these gods were meeting their needs. People embraced worshipping gods because religion is part of human life. It is uncommon to see someone who does not have a religion or believe in something.

Loyalty to the king and the entire society was enforced and guaranteed through the belief in gods. Also, people were afraid to do evil or engage in any societal disapproved behaviour because of the fear of being killed by god. Such gods in Yoruba society in those days, include, Ogun, Sango, Aiyelala, Leron, Osi, Oya, Osun, to mention a few. The traditional society enjoyed relative peace because of the efficacy of some of these gods. The entire misdemeanour that characterized the society today were uncommon in those days. Let us take stealing for example, if anyone engaged in stealing another man's property and the owner took the matter before god in those days, it was a matter of some days, the thief would die. If you committed an act and you are trying to deny, and god is contacted over the matter, it was a matter of days, the secret would come out in a disastrous way.

With the advent of Christianity and Islam a lot of people were converted. People started to put their trust in God rather than the man made gods as people were made to call them. People discovered that God is slow to anger, that he give room for sinners to repent, thus, they continue to do evil. All sort of behaviours that were detrimental to socio-economic and political development are so rampant in the society today. The Christianity/Islamism that most people embraced today is only in the mouth not in practice. That is the reason why the society seems unsafe to live in.

One shortcoming observed in the system of government led by kings was lack of accountability. The kings were in no way accountable to anybody for their stewardship. Whatever proceeds or income realised from the sales of land, tributes, royalties belong to the king. No one has the audacity to ask them to give account, unlike the situation with the modern government (democracy) which emphasises accountability from the leader. Monarchical system of government did not entail this principle.

In conclusion, Nigerians had been involved in one form of government or the other through which they ensured a peaceful society before the advent of the British colonialists, and it is important to stress that the modern system of government (Democracy) has some elements of this traditional system of government introduced with the system or carried into the system by Nigerians.

The Coming of the British

The British came to West Africa for many reasons. These reasons are economic, political, religious and social.

Economically, the British needed labour to work in their mines and plantations in the West Indies. The sugarcane plantations and mines were facing acute shortage of manpower. This problem became more pronounced as the Red Indies who are the aborigines of the place were incapable of working for hours in the farm. The Europeans generally decided to seek for labourers from West Africa. West Africans were known to be very strong and capable of working for hours on the farm. This belief about African strength was confirmed when some West Africans were taken to Europe and tested in the plantations. These West Africans worked like machines. In fact, this made the Europeans to tag them as people possessing horse power.

The Europeans lured the West Africans, especially kings and chiefs into trade in human beings. They enticed the traditional rulers with European products like gin, mirror, umbrella, perfume, to mention a few. Initially, it was the criminal or those who had broken the law of the community that were sold by the kings and chiefs but as the appetite of the kings and chiefs increased for European goods and access to fire arms, hunt for slaves increased. Villages were now invaded to capture people to be sold into slavery.

Politically, Europeans wanted to colonise Africans so as to impose their authority on them. It was believed that if Africans could be subdued and brought under control of the European government, they would be able to control the African economy. By the 18th century, the British had tactfully signed treaties with the traditional rulers in various parts of Nigeria. Where the traditional ruler failed to do this voluntarily, they were forced to do it against their will. Some traditional rulers were disposed, for this reason. Examples of disposed kings were Etsu of Nupe, Altahiru (Amir-al-mumini of Sokoto) Ovonramwen (Oba of Benin) to mention a few.

The Europeans: They had the intention of conquering Africans and establish their hegemony over them and convert the African territory. The British pursued the achievement of this policy vigorously with their military might and capability because, they were conscious of the fact that political factor controls the economic, social, religious and in fact all other human factors. That is, he who has the political power has it all. They were faced with stiff resistance in various parts of Africa especially from the traditional rulers and the people. But due to the level of their traditional advancement and military superiority, they were able to subdue all forms of resistance and bring the areas of their interest under control.

Religious Reason: The British had an erroneous belief that Africans had no knowledge of the true God and thus, they worship idols and man-made gods. They wanted to Christianize Africans by introducing Jesus Christ to them. The project of Christianizing Africans was accompanied with the introduction of western education. Establishment of church went hand in hand with that of school. Education was used as an instrument of conversion to Christianity.

Indeed, it was wrong to say that the Africans or Nigerians had no knowledge of the true God before the advent of Christianity or Islamism. The point is that the way of worship was not the same, but they belief in the supreme God as the Creator of heaven and earth were already crucial in the minds of Africans. They believed that this Supreme God is so great and so high that one has to approach Him through an intermediary. That explains why the worship of gods like Ogun, Oya, Sango, to mention a few, was so rampant among Nigerians in those days. These gods were used to instil obedience and morality in the people. The societal norms, values and beliefs were perpetually maintained and sustained through the existence and efficacy of these gods.

The society was peaceful and free from all criminalities that characterise the modern society. People would not steal or engage in any anti-social behaviour because of fear of being killed by god. When the god was contacted for any wrong doing in those days, especially to find out who had done an act, the judgement would come very fast. Apart from being contacted, the gods on their own killed, made sick or caused evil doer to confess any wrong against the fellow human being or society.

It was not uncommon in those days to see a swollen person put under bondage for wrong doings by gods, confessing his wrong doings. Some died in the process while others survived it after true confessions might have been made. The gods were contacted, appeased with sacrifice or rituals.

Social reason: The British came to clear or confirm the guesses, beliefs, scepticisms and speculations that Africans are black monkeys, uncivilised and affected in their reasoning by their colour. They wanted to come and socialise Africans.

In conclusion, it must be stressed that the Europeans came primarily for political and economic reasons while all other reasons are secondary, the motives to overthrow traditional authorities, subjecting the entire African continent under their control so as to guarantee direct access to the resources embedded in Africa and channelling than to developing their own economy was paramount in their minds.

The British had ruled Nigeria for years before the consciousness or awareness on the part of Nigeria for self government. The movement for self government or self determination was not unanimously pursued or supported by all Nigerians. For instance, the northerners insisted that they preferred British rule to self rule, and thus they distant themselves from this movement. The controversy that this movement generated resulted in the withdrawal from the legislative house by the northerners during the pre-independence era.

CHAPTER THREE: ENTHRONEMENT OF DEMOCRACY IN NIGERIA

What is Democracy?

Demos Kratia, or democracy as it is used today, means "the people rule". It is popularly defined as the government of the people, by the people and for the people. It is a kind of government in which certain people are empowered by the masses to represent their interest in the political business of administering, coordinating, directing, regulating and overseeing human affairs. In a democratic society, everybody has equal right to participate in government. Though the level of participation may not be the same for example, some people evolve themselves to the point of holding elective or nominative offices, while others participate at the level of voting for the candidates of their choice during election. It is not an aberration to see some people who would want to abstain from politics or demonstrate lack of interest to participate in government. For example, some people, due to one reason or the other decide not to register and vote during elections. Some even claim that they detest politics but whether by omission or commission, these people still participate in politics. This is so because they live in human society, they talk about electricity, good hospital, motor able roads, good salary or wages and good school to mention a few. All these things are provided by the government.

Man is a political animal, when a man fails to participate in politics or an election for whatever reason; we refer to this as political alienation. In a democratic nation, government is run by the people of that country through elections and representation. There is equality of every citizen in democracy and right to vote and make decision.

Origin of Democracy

The origin of democracy can be traced back to about 2500 years ago, and the first countries of the world to practice democracy are Athens, Greece, Rome and later America. The way democracy was practised initially is different from the way it is being practised today. Formerly, when there was a vital political decision to be taken, the whole people of the town would have to gather, each person airing his opinion. This ancient democratic method was later modernised into electing few people to take decisions on behalf of others. The modern method is advantageous over the old one because where a whole community gather over an issue; a whole day may be spent without making headway. This is due to the fact that everyone would want to express his opinion, also, the problem of space especially for a large community. People of a community or geographical zone could still express their political, social and economic opinions through their elected representatives in modern democracy.

There are many features of democracy. Most of these features are the same, but individual country use variations of main ideas. The main features which determine true democracy are:

i. **Competitive elections**: There is usually more than one political party contesting for power;

ii. Certain established rules or procedures are always in place to guide and monitor the behaviour of the major players;

iii. The pressure groups e.g. labour union, students union, and other non-governmental organisations are autonomous from government control. This is to enable them fight for the people's right;

iv. The media e.g radio, television, newspapers and magazines enjoy some degree of autonomy, this is to enhance objectivity in their reporting;

v. The representative assembly (the legislature) has some form of control over the executive but the judiciary is independent of both the legislative and executive. This is necessary to enable it dispense justice without fear or favour;

vi. One citizen one vote principle is highly adhered to.

As earlier said, there is variation in the way individual nation practises democracy. In essence, it may be difficult to see two nations who are completely homogenous or uniform in the way they practise their democracy. Some countries are highly democratised to the extent that they adhere strictly to the rule of law, ensure decentralisation of power, and give recognition to the tiers of government as well as their functions. This is true of US, UK, Canada, France, Germany etc.

Any close look at democracy in African nations would find out that there are great differences between the way democracy is practised or being practised in developed nations of the world and the way it is being practised in Africa. The reasons for this are numerous.

Firstly, the African culture which placed absolute power into the hands of the traditional rulers seems to have been incorporated into African democracy. The executive carries too much power in African democracy.

Secondly, democracy has not been firmly rooted in Africa due to corrupt civilian government which leads to incessant military seizure of power and bad military orientation that makes ambition to rule, a target of almost every individual soldier.

Thirdly, the constitution of most African nations are highly influenced by their former colonial masters or drawn under the supervision of a military junta who ensured that the constitution was prepared in such a way that would make his ambition to be life president and the richest person in the world achievable.

Fourthly, the transfer or carry-over of traditional attitude or belief that leaders are semi-god into western democracy is another reason. Ideally, in democracy, the leader is supposed to be the servant of the people as he derives his mandate and power from the masses that elected him. The situation is not so in African democracy as people elected into public offices see themselves as semi-gods who are free to do whatever they likes.

The African culture, which is the product of African idiosyncrasy, has strongly affected the respect for the rule of law which is the bedrock of democracy. The rule of law emphasises equality of individuals before the law. It ensures that individuals within a given state or country are under the law and would suffer the same punishment for the same offence committed.

Also, the rule of law makes it obligatory on every citizen whether holding public offices or not to obey court orders as well as the judgement pronounced by the court. It is the rule of law that makes the mediatory role of the judiciary to be possible. If people are free to accept or reject court order, the court will not be able to perform its duties. Though, when judgement is pronounced by the lower court, the individual has the right to appeal to the higher court, if he or she feels that the case was not properly judged. But where a judgement was pronounced by the court and the culprit did not appeal and failed to obey the judgement because of his wealth or position in the country and the court cannot force him to obey, democracy is being threatened.

Cases of disobedience to court order and outright disrespect for the rule of law are not only common but rampant in

African democracy. This has not only brought the authenticity of African democracy into question but has also created academic controversies and problems. For example, there are some things a lecturer of Citizenship Education or Political Science would tell the students in theory and the students who are conversant with the societal phenomenon would say no, it is not practicable. Let us take the immunity of some public officers e.g. Governors as an example. The Nigerian constitution like the constitution of most countries of the world forbids the arrest of any serving governor for any reason. If this is taught in our academic institutions today, it would lead to serious controversy between the lecturer and the students, because the Governor of Anambra State, in person of Dr. Ngige was not only arrested by his political god-father in conjunction with the police but was also detained for a whole day without any drastic consequence.

Apart from the above, there were series of cases where the court gave order and the government in power refused to obey and nothing followed. The worst was the situation where some individuals who had impoverished the nation through their corrupt practices while in office and who seems to be richer than the country claimed to be above the law. The event at Oputa Panel that was set up to look into the human right violations during the military rule in Nigeria, whereby some ex-military leaders were summoned to appear before the panel and they refused totally that the panel had no right to summon them, was a clear case of disrespect for the rule of law, and individuals seeing themselves to be above the law and the nation

Democracy and Nigerian Politicians

Nigerian politicians are Nigerians who have chosen politics as a vocation. It is a fact that human beings are political animals. Though, one may not participate directly in Politics that is, refusing to register and vote during an election or campaign for anybody because of his personal reason that is not enough reason to exclude him from being a politician. Consciously or unconsciously, man engages in politics. For instance, there is rarely any human being who does not need electricity, good accommodation, motor able roads, good health service, good education to mention a few. All these are needed by man and provided by the government for their subjects. There is no way an individual can adequately provide most of them. It is possible for an individual to participate in the production of some of them but the government has to give the direction and guidelines.

No man is an island; man lives in the midst of other men and needs others to live a purposeful and an accomplished life. There cannot be a society without a leader. The leader is like a pilot in a ship or plane; he determines the speed, the route and controls the ship/plane to its destination. Every society is made up of people who share the same culture, tradition, languages and who agreed on common goals and objectives. That is to say in essence that every society has a societal goal which it stands strongly to achieve (Asoga-Allen, 2001).

Before any society can form or develop her goals, there must be agreement between its inhabitants and this agreement would later transform or form the basis for selecting who is to lead the society. It is factual that everyone in the society likes to be a leader but not everyone can be a leader. For one to be a leader, he must possess certain leadership traits or qualities. These include honesty, integrity, wisdom, firmness, verbal skill, sympathy/compassion, tolerance, caring, intelligence and adaptability. He must not be selfish or claim to be wiser than others. He must not be hot tempered, partial, and must be free from bias and prejudice. He must be able to see his people as one and equal. Also, he must be able to subordinate his self-interest to the national interest. Every individual or human being has self interest but for the purpose of ensuring unity, progress, stability and cooperation in the society, everyone owes it a duty to subsume self-interest under the national interest. That is to say, the national interest is far above individual interest. It is generally believed that individuals that make the society must kill or suppress the spirit of self, if the society must make progress or achieve the societal goals. Logically speaking, what makes a nation great is more of the right minded and highly spirited individuals in that society who are strongly determined to make the state succeed rather than create wealth for themselves. Experience has shown that no matter the economic resources available in a state, if there are no honest leaders or individuals who are willing to harness the resources for a common good of all citizens, the nation would remain poor.

Some countries of the world have few economic resources and they are still very rich, since they manage the resources adequately and utilize them for the common good. In the same vein, we have countries that are well endowed with numerous economic resources but due to selfish and unpatriotic type of leaders ruling those countries, they are rated among the poorest nations of the world. This is true of Nigeria. It is highly incredible that Nigeria with all the resources at its disposal was ranked as the 15th poorest nation of the world by the United Nations in its human development index in 2004. In a state where everybody is self centred and always thinks about self rather than thinking about the generality of the people, the societal goals would suffer neglect. Where the leaders struggle for themselves rather than for the masses who elected them, there would be emergence of corrupt individuals who are richer than the state which they control.

The orientation of Nigerian politicians is really very bad. Politicians' ambition in Nigeria is far from what it is in developed nations of the world. The motives for seeking elective offices in countries like United Kingdom, United States of America, Greece, to mention a few, where democracy has brought economic greatness and technological advancement is not the same with those of Nigerian politicians. As observed by Asoga-Allen (2000)

"Nigerians want to practise the American type of democracy but cannot make the sacrifice which Americans made which led to the success of democracy in America. "

For example, it is obvious from the ways Americans go about their politics that the ultimate ambition of every American is to see America develop more than any nation of the world by allowing national interest to override self-interest.

The difference between Nigerian and American politicians is the interest. An American politician is determined to see that when we talk of nations in the world, his nation should be *primus interpres* that is first among equals.

While the majority if not all Nigerian politicians think about self interest, how to be the greatest and wealthiest person in the world and struggle ruthlessly to achieve this at the detriment of the masses that elected them. Most of them achieve this by accumulating wealth illegally. Some are richer than the state they governed and accumulated wealth that their 15th generation cannot exhaust. Political ideology of people in developed nations differs completely from what it is in the developing countries e.g. African countries. When a Nigerian politician is seeking elective position, he gives the impression that he is going there to serve his people but after getting there, he ends up serving himself and his family by diverting the resources of the nation to his personal uses mindless of what happens to the people that elected him.

Political appointment is seen by most Nigerian politicians as opportunity to corruptly enrich themselves rather than to serve their nation. An American or Briton would prefer to serve his people with all his strength and have his name written in golden record of his nation. Bill Clinton was a onetime American President who ruled America for more than seven years. As at the time he left office as President, he had no estate, no magnificent building or plane of his own or any special wealth accumulated for himself. A Councillor of local government in Nigeria who stayed in office for three years boast of establishing a fuel station that costs millions of naira, chain of cars and fertile bank accounts let alone a Local Government Chairman, Governor or President.

During the Second Republic in Nigeria (1979 - 1983), the politicians impoverished the nation by diverting the nation's resources to their personal uses. In spite of the fact that the military government that handed over to this civilian government handed over a reasonable amount of about Eight Billion Naira which as at that time was a huge amount of money, no sooner was this regime came on board than the whole money was squandered and lavished. The government went borrowing without anything to show for it. Corruption at that period in the nation reached an alarming proportion that more than nine legislators purchased Jet planes for themselves in addition to a chain of expensive luxurious cars. The level of poverty among the masses during this regime and open displayed of wealth by politicians led to military coup that swept away the government. Though, there had been corruption before the advent of the Second Republic but it was not as pronounced and significantly displayed as in the Second Republic.

The situation in the Second Republic opened the eyes of the successive military administration except that of General Buhari/Idiagbon to the issue of corruption. Governance in Nigeria was now a matter of acquisition of illegal wealth and the Nigerian masses started groaning in poverty and penury, while the leaders were busy stocking the nation's money in foreign banks for themselves and their families (Asoga-Allen, 2000). The problem of corruption among Nigerians is a chronic one according to Oyeneye (1997). There is corruption both in low and high places. If there is corruption in low places today, one may say it is as a result of flagrant display of ill gotten wealth by those on the top.

Today, people say the nation's economy is in a shamble bad state, that the nation has economic problem. If we should put things right, the nation's problem is not that of economy but the people. The reason for this is that there was no year in which the income of the nation depreciated from what it used to be in the previous years. In essence, the nation's income appreciates yearly except for the recent global economic meltdown. There were instances where the income exceeded the one budgeted for but this had not transformed to improvement in the condition of living of the people. Civilian ruled the nation; the story is that of abject poverty of the masses and emergence of few millionaire politicians. Military came under the pretext to save the situation, the situation became worse as billions of dollars earned from crude oil were diverted to personal uses. The questions are:

1. Who is going to save Nigerian masses?
2. Is Nigeria going to continue this way in the hands of unscrupulous, unpatriotic, selfish and self-centred few Nigerians?
3. Who is even clean now to rule Nigeria as corruption has eaten deep into the bones and marrows of Nigerians?
4. What is the way out of this problem of corruption in Nigeria?

It is impracticable and impossible to expect somebody from another planet to rule Nigeria. Nigerians will continue to rule Nigeria. The salvation of Nigerians is in their own hands, the earlier we change the better. The way things are going on in this part of the world is very dangerous and capable of causing chaos and anarchy, most especially when people are pushed to the wall. God does not want the death of a sinner but to repent. But in a situation where a sinner continues to sin and refuses to repent, the outcome would be death. According to the Biblical injunction, it is righteousness that exalts a nation; sin is a reproach to a people. Also, it is obvious that we cannot continue in sin and expect the glory of God to abound.

Whoever is in power today or in future should bear it in mind that Nigerians cannot continue this way for ever. People will not watch helplessly and hopelessly forever, while the resources of the nation are being shared and diverted by just a few individuals. One day, the people would be tired of what they are going through and would be willing to resist the oppressive, selfish and corrupt government. This resistance may open the book of history as those who contributed to the situation the nation and her people are finding themselves would find themselves to blame. This may be dangerous for such leaders and their families whether at home or abroad. French revolution emanated from injustice and oppression which the bourgeoisies subjected the common people to then in France.

In Nigeria today, it is difficult to say or point out somebody as a clean person. This is because the whole society is in a mess. Since people who made it through crooked ways have been displaying and enjoying their wealth, the generality of the people have changed their mentality towards acquisition of wealth. Unlike the situation under African traditional setting where people cherish their names than riches and gold, today, a lot of people are ready to do anything just to make it. The situation is so worse that even among those who claim to be ministers of God; you rarely find any who does not cherish money than the gospel he claims God called him to preach. What I am saying in essence is that the problem of corruption in Nigeria does not leave out houses of God. Who then is to be trusted?

The way out of corruption must come from the top. The day that the nation is fortunate to have a God fearing leader, who is not avaricious and self-centred, the problem of the nation would start to have solution. If a leader with clean hands emerges, he would be able to make drastic laws that would wash the society of bad eggs. Though, to clean Nigeria of corruption, one should expect blood to flow. Mere imprisonment cannot hamper people from corruption. Similar offences should carry similar penalties. For example, in Nigeria, armed robbery is an offence that carries death penalty. But there is need to stress here that there is no difference between armed robbery and pen robbery. When you robbed a person of his belongings with arms, the owner of the properties may be killed in the process or after either by the armed robber or the shock received from the exercise or feelings of the colossal lost sustained from the exercise. In the same vein, somebody who used pen to rob the nation or country of millions or billions of naira has caused serious financial inconveniences on millions of the citizens. We have seen in the past where a lot of children died of deficiency of balanced diet due to poor feeding. When something that belongs to the masses is pocketed by a single person, he has indirectly killed others who supposed to benefit from it.

Pen robbery carries heavier weight than armed robbery because the amount involved in pen robbery is higher than that of armed robbery, pen robbers have been treated with integrity in Nigeria when compared to his counterpart; armed robbers, perhaps, because of the categories of people engage in both. Those who engaged in armed robbery in most cases are frustrated people who have no job and are tired of life, but on the other side you find highly placed people who are entrusted with the wealth of the nation. The earlier we recognise that armed robbery and pen robbery are the same offence and give them the same punishment, the better for the nation.

Democracy and Nigerian Masses

Nigerians generally, like democracy as a system of government and they want democracy to be practised in Nigeria because it is a system of government that ensures mass participation of people in government and also, it confers on the people power to decide on whom to elect to represent their interest in government. Nigerian masses are beginning to lose interest in the process of electing leaders in the country. A lot of Nigerians have lost their conscience due to injustice that is so rampant in the country during elections and the failure of previously elected politicians to fulfil their electoral promises. Unlike the situation in the past where people were enthusiastically moved to participate in the registration and voting during elections, a lot of people were reluctant to register, some that registered refused to vote because they lack confidence in the system. It is a common saying among the people that whether you vote or not, the election would still be rigged. People become discourage when an election does not produce the true result or represent the true decision of the masses. Majority of Nigerian voters have sold their conscience by collecting money or gift before going to vote. Most dubious politicians in Nigeria use money to buy the conscience of voters. They do this in the first place because they lack confidence in themselves and secondly because their major motive for seeking elective offices is to corruptly enrich themselves. The motive to loot the treasury made politics in Nigeria a do or die affair. If the motive is to serve the people and one loses an election one would have to accept his or her fate. But that is not usually the case. Many Nigerian politicians make use of thugs, assassins, charms and other dangerous weapons to oppress their opponents.

Most Nigerian is suffering from political immaturity. They engage in money politics. They believe that they must be settled before they go and vote. And when they are given a token like two hundred naira (N200) they forget about the credibility of the person that is offering them money and they proceed to vote him into office. Before and during election, politicians distribute food stuff, money, electrical gadgets to entice people to vote for them. Politicians spend billions of naira in Nigeria for an election and when the election is won, they concentrate on how to recover their money rather than on how to give the people dividends of democracy. When electorates complain of non-performance of the elected leaders, the leaders shun them because they believe that the service rendered to them by the masses by voting them into office had been paid for. Thus, the masses have no reason to complain.

The level of poverty may have accounted for this ugly situation. It is obvious that the nation is blessed with abundant natural resources and Nigeria is said to be 6th largest producer of crude oil in the world, but there is not much development to show for the income from crude oil. This is as a result of large scale corruption from those entrusted with the management of the national resources. The leaders have been possessed by the spirit of self and care not about those that elected them. No wonder, people are ready to accept a loaf of bread from the politician before voting for him. A lot of Nigerians are jobless; they are not employed even though they are employable. Those that are employed are paid poor salaries that are insufficient for them to meet the needs of their immediate families. Many Nigerian workers were not able to change their shoes or even feed well before the advent of third Republic. The third Republic made a little difference by preparing what could be called living salary/wages for Nigerian workers. The joy of this was short-lived as the same regime started to embark on periodic increase in prices of petroleum and petroleum products which affected the standard of living negatively. Prices of food stuff skyrocketed, house rent went up, transportation and others become unaffordable.

The political situation of Nigeria today is such that only the rich can win in an election. No matter your intelligence and educational attainment, if you have no money, you cannot be voted for in Nigeria. That is the reason why the same group of people revolve every time in Nigerian politics. The Nigerian masses are yet to be conscious of the fact that the money being used by these politicians are the nation's money which they illegally acquired. They are being given what is their own for them to render extra service. Assuming the money is not from the nation's treasury, the fact that somebody offers bribe to induce people into voting for him is enough to disqualify such a person. It is evidence that, that type of person has nothing to offer, he is a fake and bloody rogue.

This problem of offering money to the masses to buy their conscience is a serious one in Nigerian democracy. Except it is checked, right people may never ascend the throne of leadership in Nigeria.

Those who serve as thugs and assassins for Nigerian politicians are from Nigerian masses. Most of the politicians keep their wards in expensive universities in United States of America, United Kingdom and some other developed nations and hire the children of the poor to serve as thugs and assassins. Apart from not having the required capital, most decent Nigerians are not willing to come and seek elective offices in Nigerian politics because of the ways and manners politics is being played. To most reasonable and responsible Nigerians, politics is a dirty game. But to my mind, politics is a good vocation, only the way it is played in Nigeria that is dirty and crude. The crudity in Nigerian politics is due to the motives Nigerian politicians carried into the game. If the motive is to serve the people, the game would not be a do or die one. Since people have the motive of enriching themselves, they are ready to do anything to get there.

People equate leadership with wealth. The mentality of the people is based on the faulty idiosyncrasy. This has affected everyone in Nigerian society both young and old, Christians and Muslims, and even traditional religionists are not exempted. Before the advent of the British colonialists in Nigeria, the people had a way by which the society was governed. For example, in the western part of Nigeria, we had monarchical system of government headed by the Obas. In the east, we had Obis or Igwes and in the northern part of the country we had Emirs. These traditional rulers were unquestionable to anyone as regards the ways and manners they executed their politics. They are so powerful that they could do and undo. Apart from being in charge of the wealth of their kingdoms/Emirates, they had power to seize the wife/daughter of their subject for marriage without any query. This was largely true of Yoruba land where the Obas had absolute control and authority over the people. Corruption in modern system of government called democracy could be said to be a carryover or transfer of value from primitive or traditional concept to the modern system.

Democracy does not emphasise acquisition of wealth for elected leadership, and nations where democracy have triumphed, the philosophy of governance is not based on accumulation of wealth for the leaders but for the nation and for the benefits of all the citizens. Democracy is people oriented government not individualistic or dictatorship, and the place of sound economy as a pre-requisite to successful democracy cannot be overemphasised. Think of any nation where democracy is firmly rooted when the economy is in shamble. Indeed, it may be rightly said that the fuel for democratic machine is sound economy. Sound national economy is enhanced when the intention of everyone works towards the success of the nation and the common good of all. That is exactly what is conspicuously absent in Nigerian democracy. And this is the major reason for the failure of democracy. The feeling of the people is that politics is a vocation that makes people rich overnight. That is, no sooner you are sworn in after election that you become a multi-millionaire. This mentality makes people struggle for what they can get from the nation, not what they can contribute to the nation. Everyone struggles to take his own portion of the national cake. Even where a politician came into the office with the ambition to serve the people with a honest mind, this decision would soon change by the time his people start to remind him that this is his time and no one held his office in the past and came out poor. As observed by Asoga-Allen (2000)

"When any Nigerian is appointed into public office, the first thing his friends and relations would tell him is that, this is your time, nobody held that position before and was poor. That is telling him directly or indirectly that he has to acquire wealth by all means".

This mentality is the mother of tribal politics. In Nigeria today, it is customary for every tribe to cry of marginalisation. The reason for this is that people do not focus governance from the telescope of selfless service but from the perspective of self aggrandizement and self benefit. What Nigerians need is good governance not the ethnic origin of the president. This clamouring is attributable to the impression that the ethnic group of the president would be favoured in terms of political appointments, provision of social amenities and infrastructural facilities. Democracy should be for equal opportunities for all citizens. The idea of having every tribe producing the nation's president is not bad, but whoever want to be president must struggle and be popular among all the tribes and also, he must be noted for intellectual capability and flair for administration. Selection of president should be based on the antecedent of the individual contesting for it in terms of social, economic, political, religious and educational attainments. That is the only way to guide against the emergence of a mediocre, local and incompetent person as president. Any tribe that feels marginalised should be asked to produce a national candidate or consensus candidate. If that is done, such a tribe should be supported because it is dangerous to give the impression that some tribes cannot be president in a nation that is practising democracy. Such idea would violate the ideals of democracy.

In conclusion, if democracy must succeed in Nigeria, people must shun traditional attitudes, beliefs that equate leadership with acquisition of wealth at the detriment of the people and the national interest and imbibe the culture of democracy which emphasises equal opportunities for all citizens. Placement of national interest above self interest, detribalisation, accountability, competence, probity, Self-centredness, acquisition of wealth illegally, using force to pacify others not to express their feelings about leadership atrocities, placing oneself above the law and lack of respect for the rule of law are foreign to democracy and contrary to democratic ideals. Unless Nigerians struggle seriously to overcome all these attitudinal problems, democracy is bound to fail.

Nigerian Democracy and Nigerian Economy

It is pertinent to conceptualise the term economy under this sub-heading before delving into how Nigerian democracy affect positively or negatively or both the nation's economy. And the implications of democracy built on weak or poor economy.

Economy according to Asoga-Allen (2003) can be defined in many or various ways for example, it can be defined as a system by which a country's money and goods are produced or the means by which a county produces wealth and acquire those things it cannot produce. Economy can also be defined as the careful use of money time, goods etc so that nothing is wasted. One can also define economy as something that is done in order to spend less money. It is the means by which a country derives its income, because a country derives its income through production of goods and services. No country in the world whether developed or developing can claim to be self-sufficient. This is because no country is capable of producing all her needs.

Economically, a country produces in surplus quantity the goods in which it has comparative advantage over others and exchanges them with other countries who produce in large quantity what it cannot produce. This process is referred to as international trade. The law of comparative cost or advantage states that a country should specialise in the production of a particular good which he is able to produce more cheaply and efficiently than the others. This policy of specialisation brings comparative advantages to the individual country. Apart from making goods of other countries available to those countries that cannot produce them or produce them in insufficient quantity, it also serves as a source of foreign exchange earnings.

When we talk of economic resources, we simply mean the various sources from which a country derives its income. Nigerian economic resources include crude oil, timber, coal, cocoa, palm oil, groundnut, cassava, bitumen, gas, to mention a few. The nation's economy depends largely on the available resources which it is endowed with, the technological know-how in tapping the resources effectively and efficiently as well as adequate management and utilization of income accruing from the resources for national development and common good of man. Where this is properly managed it leads to economic boom or buoyancy and where it is improperly managed, it results in poor economy.

That a nation is blessed with numerous mineral resources is not enough to make her a prosperous nation. There is need for technological know-how in terms of exploration and exploitation of the resources and when this has been successfully developed, the next equally important stage is that of honest, patriotic and reliable leaders to manage the economy. This explains mostly why many African countries are blessed with abundant mineral resources and people are still wallowing in poverty as against some western countries though, do not have many resources but, the little they have are properly managed and diverted to the areas of national needs.

The joy in the system of government a state adopts is in the ability of the system to affect the lives of citizens positively. That is, how the system brings about economic viability and prosperity. The economy of a system of government is what makes it worthy of adoption. No nation would want to adopt a system of government that seems to impoverish the people and cannot guarantee economic prosperity and stability. In the same vein, it must be stressed that no system of government can adopt and practice itself; it is the people that adopts it and determines its workability. Basically, democracy has brought about economic viability and an all round development in most developed countries of the world. The successes achieved through the system were due to determination, commitment and patriotism on the part of the leaders and founders of those countries.

Nigeria is a democratic state whether counterfeit or genuine but looking at the way things had been going in the country, there is rarely any good thing one can point to as the product of democracy. All what could be said about democracy in Nigeria is that it makes those who hold public offices (politicians) to be rich overnight and the masses to lavish in the cell of poverty and penury. It is a fact that democracy had not been allowed to stay long in Nigeria due to highly corrupt government run by Nigerian politicians who had given the military the opportunity to penetrate the wall of government and rule the nation. Ironically, military government had turned out to be more corrupt than the civilian government, as the government favoured the emergence of individual billionaires among the military leaders.

Democracy is being run in Nigeria as a very expensive government. The public office holders earn salaries that make one feels that their ambition is to share the resources of the country rather than to develop the country as they claim. Unnecessary offices are created to give opportunity to party loyalists to be part of the government. The executives at the federal, state and local governments have crops of advisers who earn fabulous salaries every month. Apart from this, ministries are duplicated just to have people appointed as commissioners and ministers. If the aim of the leaders is to ensure good life for the people and buoyant economy for the nation, the strength of the economy has to be taken into consideration when appointing and considering the number of offices to be created.

Resources of the nation are wasted on projects that have no direct bearing in the lives of the people. For instance, the sum of sixty billion naira (N60, 000,000,000) was spent by Obasanjo's regime to build Abuja Stadium in year 2003. To many rational people, this was a waste. One would have expected such money to be used as loans for millions of school leavers and graduates of Nigerian higher institutions who were jobless. There is National Stadium in Lagos which belongs to the Federal Government. This should have served the purpose for which Abuja Stadium was hurriedly built at that time. At the state level, public fund are directed towards building for the rich and not for the poor. Government claim that they are building houses for the masses but after building the houses, their prices became so exorbitant for the poor, they are sold for five million naira (N5, 000,000) and above how many Nigerians can afford five hundred thousand naira not to talk of five million naira? If government really wants to help the people, why not give them land with loan to build houses of their choice?

In the name of democracy, fake contracts were awarded to fake contractors and the money collected by those who awarded them. Some contracts were genuinely awarded but were not executed and the money were collected and shared between those who awarded it and the awardees. Similar to this, is the inflation of contract fees. All these are done for self interest. That is the reason why Nigerian economy is in a mess. These fraudulent activities are not peculiar to democratic government in Nigeria, but also military government. There was a particular military leader that legalised corruption, and called it "shop I shop". No wonder about twelve billion dollars realized from crude oil during the Gulf war which took place during his regime was embezzled. The only record available to the government showed that he only imported sardine for the forces from the loan he obtained from a foreign country during his regime.

As a result of corrupt practices of the leaders, people remain poor. Most of the leaders became richer than the country that they ruled. Since the second Republic, government in Nigeria engages in one economic measure or the other. These have brought untold hardship on the people and never recorded any economic development. For instance, The Structural Adjustment Programme (SAP), Austerity Measure (AM), Devaluation of Currency (DC), removal of subsidies on petroleum products, feeding of Nigerian students in higher institutions, students hostels, and so on and so forth are different names used for different measures adopted at different times. Ironically, the masses suffered the result of all these economic measures. The government did not reduce her own spending that is, what individual public office holders spent to maintain - his office entitlements, welfare and administration. But what the masses enjoyed was stopped.

Apart from the above, people only suffer for nothing at the end of the day, since the measure did not result into any meaningful economic development. They only helped in providing enough money for the leadership to spend and embezzle.

The embezzlement by political office holders reached an alarming proportion that the nation's roads became death traps. No money to repair the roads, not to talk of constructing a new one. Accidents due to bad roads were so rampant. In the education sector no adequate finance. The infrastructural facilities became decay. Lecturers in the higher institutions could not embark on research activities, students found it difficult to feed and purchase textbooks. The libraries of most Nigerian higher institutions lacked modern textbooks. To most Nigerian political office holders, education is a burden because it is capital intensive. Funding education very well would affect the treasury that is there may not be enough to steal. When the teachers/lecturers are on strike, they are less bothered because majority of them do not patronise Nigerian education market for the education of their children. They have enough money to purchase enough big houses in America, Britain, Switzerland, and so on and so forth, and they are stinking rich, they can afford to send their children to the best universities in the world.

In Nigerian concept, public schools are meant for children of the poor. That is why teachers are tagged nuisance and considered irrelevant in the society, even though, they trained those that are leading us today. The same problem of inadequate finance applies to the health sector. Most Nigerian hospitals have no drugs, the medical doctors are not well paid, the best ones struggle for foreign appointment and fly out of the country. That is the genesis of brain drain that the country is experiencing today. A lot of people who feel they cannot make it if they stay in Nigeria look for opportunities to travel out for a better job. Those that decided to stay in Nigeria were turned to corrupt officers by the economic hardship of the country. Thus, corruption becomes a household name in the country. If there was any civil servant that built a house during most regimes in Nigeria, the source of wealth of such officer would be doubtful, if he did not obtain house loan from government.

This was due to the fact that the salaries paid to public servant were too low and still too low for a worker to feed himself three times a day, pay house rent, cloth himself and his family as well as send his children to school. The situation was so bad that some Permanent Secretaries in the past retired to a rented quarters. Today, because of the fear of how to cope with life after retirement, most workers are corrupt. They struggle for what they can use their offices to benefit from the government, not what they can contribute to the government. Gratuities after retirement cannot earn the retirees a good business. In the process of collecting it, some lost their lives. This is because years after retirement most people find it difficult to collect their entitlements. We have seen instances where people collapsed and died during verification exercises in the past. It is the feeling of the people that unless they made it before retirement they would suffer.

Corruption does not exclude those in the private sector and even the artisans. People deal with one another fraudulently. Go to mechanic workshop with your car, some of the mechanics would tell you what is not bad is bad. If you give them the benefit to work on your car while you are away for another pressing business, some good part of your car may be replaced with a bad one so that the good ones could be sold back to you as a replacement. All other artisans, e.g. bricklayers, carpenter, bicycle repairer, painters, to mention a few, also engages in one corrupt practice or the other.

Market women are not left out of corruption in Nigeria. Most of the time measurements are falsified to cheat the buyer. Fake products are sometimes sold as original one to unsuspecting buyers. Many importers, import fake products. Go to Nigerian market and see large number of fake electrical and electronic goods. In fact, this is really horrible as you can rarely find a genuine product again in the market. You buy a new antenna after fixing, it does not work, you buy a new television, it does not last two weeks, before developing a fault. Some old products are painted and sold as new while the inside components are already old. Righteousness to most Nigerians is foolishness. People want to get to a desired end through whatever means they feel would lead them there. What people want to hear is that he has made it not how he made it.

The economic situation of Nigeria calls for a serious attention to save the country from imminent danger. The young ones seem to have no future. Millions of Nigerian graduates are jobless and they are being asked to create job, even though they were not given money. Even, in the oil producing states, the story is the same. There is youth restiveness which has resulted into incessant riot in places like Warri, Port Harcourt and many others. Oil workers are sometimes kidnapped for weeks. Some lost their lives in the process. The situation is so bad that people are praying that the oil should dry up so that they can enjoy their natural environment which had already been bastardized and degraded due to oil exploration and exploitation. In the light of the above, it is obvious that it is not well with Nigeria economically and politically. The political class controls the economic factor and formulates economic policies for every nation. Where political policies do not affect the economy positively, there is political and economic problem.

When Nigeria was under regional government and each region was allowed to decide for itself and her people, there was a rapid development in the socio-economic, political and religious lives of the people, especially in the western region.

Reverse became the case when we started Presidential system of government and states were created. The First Republic was not allowed to exist for long before the government was toppled in a bloody coup that led to the emergence of General Aguyi Ironsi as the first Head of State and Commander in Chief of Armed Forces after which General Yakubu Gowon came in through another coup. The leadership of the country shall be discussed from the time of Yakubu Gowon till date.

In conclusion, corruption, inequality, self centeredness, misplacement of priority and poverty as a result of bad economy all constitute a great threat to democracy in Nigeria. This is so because a hungry man is an angry man, people would not cease to cry out of any bad economy as a result of bad government, more so when they are not ignorant of the income of the nation. When the crying of the people reached the climax, military opportunists are bound to seize power. No constitution can stop military coup or revolution of the great masses against any oppressive government. Only good governance can stabilize democracy in Nigeria and indeed any country.

Nigeria Democracy and the Legislators
The legislature is one of three arms of Government in the Nigerian federalism. The legislature comes under two houses namely, House of Representative and The House of Senate. The legislators are expected to be above board in character. They are expected to be people who love their country, who are determined to ensure the greatness of the country by making good laws that are capable of ensuring good condition of living for the people that elected them. In addition, they

are expected to be patriotic Nigerians who see the whole nation as their jurisdiction. They are not expected to be tribalistic, selfish or bias about any ethnic group or tribe. From all indications, it seems the Nigerian legislators have not lived to the expectation of Nigerians. They have not justified the confidence reposed on them. This is so because the issues that bother on welfare of the masses rarely arouse their interest except issues that have to do with self.

Nigerian legislators rarely call the executive to order when it is pursuing bad economic policies which brings serious economic hardship on the masses. The relationship with executive remains cordial and smooth so far the allocations are being released on time. The only time they come in conflict with the executive is when it refuses to release allocation on time or accuses any of them of wrong doing. The way Nigerians who elected them into office see them is different from the way they see themselves. They too perceive their offices as that of accumulating wealth by looting the treasury. During the Second Republic in Nigeria, the legislators did not act as check and balance to the activities of the executive; rather they cooperated with the executive to share the money in the national purse and looted the treasury. No wonder, there was never a threat of impeachment. Every day of that regime was a Christmas. No sooner they were sworn in than they emptied the treasury. Before the first four years of the regime, the nation's economy was already in a worst state. The regime had to obtain foreign loans which were not used for any developmental project but to ensure enough looting. The loans obtained by this regime in the name of the nation were still being paid till 2005. The debt had increased greatly that the nation spent billions of dollars to service it.

The loan obtained by this regime and others rose to 32 billion U.S dollars. The 60% debt forgiveness granted Nigeria by the group of eight most industrialised nations of the world called G8 reduced the nation's foreign debt to 12 billion U.S dollars owed to G8 which was agreed to be paid twice with the first coming in by September 2008. These legislators connived with the executives to loot the nation's treasury. Many of them emerged multi-millionaires and multi-billionaires. They owned expensive luxurious cars, fertile foreign accounts, while those who elected them groaned in poverty and starvation. Because of the serious economic hardship which the people were made to go through during the time and the cry of the poor, the military overthrew the government and started to rule the nation.

The third Republic legislators came on board with the same spirit with those of the second Republic. Not only that they came in to pursue self interest but were determined and over ambitious to loot the nation. Their efforts to loot the treasury like that of the second Republic legislators was thwarted by the executive who seemed not to agree to mass looting of the treasury. The refusal of the executive to support the nefarious and selfish plans of the legislators resulted into a series of attempted impeachments and threats of impeachment which tried to divert the attention of the executive from fulfilling some vital part of his electoral promises.

The first corrupt initiative of the legislators under the third republic that generated serious sensation and hullabaloo from the public was the issue of five million naira (N5, 000.000) furniture loan proposed for each legislator. This came after billions of naira had been spent by them on hotel accommodation. Nigerians generally raised serious eye brow on the development to the extent that the Nigerian workers under the Nigerian Labour Congress went to Abuja to protest the proposal. In spite of this the legislators received the money. Even though the executive had its own weaknesses, there were series of false allegations against the executive by the legislators. These were followed by the attempted impeachments which Nigerian condemned in totality and were later dropped after the executive had settled them by giving them what they really wanted. A lot of corrupt practices were perpetrated by these legislators. For instance, they collected money from members of the public who needed their assistance before rendering such. There was daily distribution of money bags in the house. A particular instance was when the ministers were being asked to bring money to have the budget for their ministries jacked up. Some ministers spent millions of naira to do this during the first four years of the third Republic headed by President Olusegun Obasanjo.

There were series of corrupt charges or allegations against the leadership of the house of Senate and house of

Representatives to the extent that the Independent Corrupt Practices Commission (ICPC) which was established by the executive and reluctantly supported by the legislators intervened several times to investigate them but instead of submitting themselves for investigation, they attempted impeaching the president. If the corruption plans of these legislators were successful the nation would have been brought back to square one as did by the second republic leaders. Thank God, the executive did not compromise. The legislators during the second tenure of the third Republic continue with the style of the legislators under the first tenure. Though, this was not a surprise since most of them are still the same people in the first tenure. Anytime their allocation was not given on time, they quickly draw impeachable offences against the president, but when allocation was being released as at when due, the president was doing well, no complaint against him.

Some of the bad actions of the legislators in the first tenure which was repeated in the second tenure led to the intervention of the executive and indeed the Agencies established against corruption. An example of such actions was the bribery collected by the Senate President in conjunction with the house committee on education from some ministers to jack up the 2005 budget of their ministries. The one that became so conspicuous was that of the former Minister of Education, Professor Fabian Osuji who gave fifty five million naira (N55, 000,000) bribe to the Senate President,

Chief Wabara and members of the House Committee on Education. That led to the removal of Chief Wabara from his post as Senate President and the sack of Fabian Osuji as Education Minister. Others who participated in the deal were also punished. They were all charged to court.

Members of the house of Assembly were very furious about the actions of the Executive whom they claimed mingled all the legislators together and tagged them as a bundle of corrupt individuals. The actions that followed were the compilation of impeachable offences which were not known before against the president. This lingered on for a long time before they became silent over it, perhaps because of the immediate release of allocation to them by the Executive. In advanced countries, when the legislators threaten to impeach the Executive, people take it very serious because they know that the President must have indeed contravened or ran contrary to certain constitutional provisions. That is, have contravened the law. But in Nigeria, nobody takes the legislators serious when they talk of impeachment. The impression that most people have when that happens is that they are fighting for their purse as there is no evidence to show that they love their country but themselves and members of their families.

In United States of America, the Congress is a very powerful body even more powerful than the executive. They cannot be taken for a ride because you cannot entice members of the Congress with money or anything. Their ultimate ambition is that America should continue to be great and remain the greatest in the whole world. Any policy that would not help the achievement of this objective will not scale through the Congress. The situation in Nigeria is different, the Executive can carry out any policy he likes whether good or bad provided he is ready to settle members of the house of Assembly. That is the reason why people see their existence in Nigeria as a waste of the nation's resources. Billions of naira is being expended to maintain the house of Assembly in Nigeria, but with less returns from the legislators. Where they need to have checked the Executive, they show non-challant attitude. The only thing that bothers them is their pockets.

There is no gainsaying that members of the house of Assembly in Nigeria are not representing anybody but themselves. They are just there as mere figure heads. Their impacts are not felt by the people that elected them.

If the legislators have been alive to their responsibilities and abstain from corruption, they would have been able to stop the Executive from embarking on economic policies that are deadly to the masses. It is true that every reform brings about pains at the beginning and if properly carried out with honesty, commitment and dedicated mind, it brings pleasure and good at the end. Economic reforms have to be planned and gradually carried out for a period of time. It should not be carried out using military approach. Economic reform should make use of economic approach. Using military approach, that is, trying to reform the economy that has been bastardized by corruption of the leaders within a short period without collecting back all what had been stolen and embarking on policies that tend to bring more hardship to already wounded individuals in the society is more deadly than helpful. To buttress this point, who are the people suffering the economic hardship which the so called economic reform is bringing on Nigerians? Those who have stolen enough from the nation's treasury can never be affected even if a litre of petrol is being sold for five hundred naira (N500.00). I don't think that even God the creator of heaven and earth can support any reform that would lead to death of many people in the name of economy improvement.

The problem of corruption, ineffectiveness and inactiveness is not peculiar to the federal legislators. Even at the state level most of the legislators put their heads permanently under the governors as if they have been bought. You can never hear them criticising any unpopular policy of the Governors. What they tell the masses is that all is correct even when the people cannot see anything on ground to justify the claim. We are not saying that the legislators should engage the Executive in a war but they are an arm of government which has the constitutional backing to stand distinctively to fight for the masses by ensuring good governance. Where the legislature is in absolute compromise with the Executive and only serves as a rubber stamp to the activities of the Executive is very dangerous to any democracy. It only usually happens where there is corruption going on between the Executive and the

Legislators. What is being said here in essence is that everyday cannot be Christmas. There should be some days when the legislators would disagree with some unpopular policies of the Executive. There is no way you can convince the masses that all the activities of the executives are rational and not based on self sentiment, prejudice or bias.

Except the Nigerian legislators change from their corrupt way of enriching themselves and imbibe the spirit of patriotism, honesty, loyalty and subjection of the spirit of self to that of the nation and devote themselves fully to the development of Nigeria, democracy can never bring any development in Nigeria. Each regime would just come eat and go, inflicting injuries on the people to enable them have enough to steal and spend under the guise of economic reform. Even, where the economic reform actually brings about economic stability during the time of a regime, what of the incoming regime? How are we sure that the incoming regime would continue on the path of his predecessor as it is usually the case in Nigeria.

In conclusion, the type of democracy expected by Nigerian masses is democracy of economic prosperity not the democracy of poverty and impoverishment that tends to make the rich to be richer through corruption and the poor to be poorer. Any democracy based on poverty, impoverishment and inequality of the citizens cannot stand the test of time. To stabilize democracy, it should not be by mere empty proclamations but should be by action, determination and genuine commitment.

CHAPTER FOUR: NIGERIAN DEMOCRACY AND THE RULE OF LAW

Principles of the Rule of Law

What is the rule of law? For much of human history, rulers and laws were synonymous. Law was simply the will of the rulers. A first step away from such tyranny was the notion of rule by law including the notion that even a ruler should rule by virtue of legal means. Democracies went further to establish the rule of law. Although no society or government system is free. rule of law are fundamental political, social and economic rights. It reminds that tyranny and lawlessness are the only alternatives. According to the United States Information Publication (2004), rule of law means that no individual, president or private citizen, stands above the law. Democratic government exercise authority by way of law and are themselves subjects to law's constraints.

Laws should express the will of the people, not the whims of kings, dictators, military officials, religious leaders, or self appointed political parties.

Citizens in democracies are willing to obey the laws of their society, then because they are submitting to their own rules and regulations. Justice is best achieved when the laws are established by the very people who must obey them.

Under the rule of law, a system of strong, independent courts should have the power and authority, resources, and the prestige to hold government officials, even top leaders, accountable to the nation's laws and regulations.

For this reason, judges should be well trained, professional, independent and impartial. To serve their necessary role in the legal and political system, judges must be committed to the principles of democracy.

Principles of democracy

The laws of democracy may have many sources: written constitutions; statues and regulations; religious and ethical techniques; and cultural traditions and practices. Regardless of origin, the law should enshrine certain provisions to protect the rights and freedom of citizens; under the requirement of law of equal protection, the law may not be uniquely applicable to any single individual or group.

Citizens must be secured from arbitrary arrest and unreasonable search of their homes or the seizure of their personal property.

Citizens charged with crimes are entitled to a speedy and public trial, along with the opportunity to confront and question their accusers, if convicted; they may not be subject to cruel or unusual punishment. Lastly, citizens cannot be forced to testify against themselves. This principle protects citizens from coercion, abuse or torture and greatly reduces the temptation of police to employ such measures.

The rule of law is the foundation on which democracy is built. It guarantees equality of every individual irrespective of the status economic and financial position in the society. To ensure that this is maintained, it recommends an independent court of law which is free from any manipulation or dictation of those in authority. The judgement pronounced in the court must be in line with the constitution or existing laws in the state. According to the principle of rule of law, the laws of the state must emanate or express the will of the people, not that of the rulers. This is necessary to guide against imposition of human or draconic laws on the people. The rationale in this is that it is believed that people would be willing to obey the law which expresses their will rather than the one that is foreign and represents the will of the ruler. Ideally, laws are made to guide people away from activities the society detests and considers inimical to the society. Every society in the world has a goal which it strives to achieve, for the effective and efficient realization of this goal, everybody must be committed and dedicated. No one should engage in any activity that can jeopardise the achievement of the goal. One of the ways of preventing anti-progress behaviour is by putting in place laws that would forbid people from acting in like manner. There may not be sin when there is no law. If there is sin, there may not be generally accepted means of punishing the offender. With the law in place, the scepticism as to whether somebody who acted in way not acceptable to the acceptable norms of society has committed an offence or not is discarded. The laws are made for man by man to guide man's behaviour positively. The laws should not be used as a trap on man. How would a law not be used as a trap? The only way that the law can be seen as a guide to human behaviour is when the law arises from the will of the majority not from few individuals. At the same time when laws are made, people need to know that such laws exist. In essence, to make law is not enough, the people that the laws are made for must be informed about the existence of such laws. It is a common saying in legal perspective that ignorance is not an excuse in the law court. But from the moral perspective, when somebody was not aware of the existence of a law before he fell victim of it, the punishment given to such person may not satisfy moral questions.

From the moral perspective, a person would be considered an offender after he has contravened a law that is well known to him. To guide against ignorance of the law, the state owes it a duty to carry out regular enlightenment through radio, television, handbills, pamphlets, newspapers, and so on and so forth. It is through adequate enlightenment programmes that people can be conscious of the existing laws. Then, the offender would have no excuse as to being ignorance of the existence of such law he contravened.

Equally important is the fact that the court should be manned by competent, highly trained professionals, independent and impartial judges. Where the rule of law is properly adhered to, the court is supposed to be fully independent of both the executives and the legislators. The situation in most African nations is that the judiciary is only independent in theory but in practice, it is not. Let us take the case of Nigeria; the appointment of judges in Nigeria is done by the President after the ratification of the legislators. Promotion of the judges must be approved by the President. Allocation of funds to the court or Ministry of Justice is done by the President. How then does one expect the judiciary to be free? It is a common saying that "he, who pays the piper, dictates the tune". That is the reason why people cannot have the assurance of getting 100% justice from the court especially when it has to do with the government. Also, the idea of strong court, that have the power and authority, resources and the prestige to hold government officials, even top leaders accountable to the nation's law and the regulations remains an illusion. This is because the court finds it difficult to bite the fingers that feed it.

The consequences of twisting the rule of law as it relates to the judiciary in Nigeria are so pronounced in the nation. And it leads people into controversies as to whether the system of government the nation is practising is democracy or not. The general belief among most Nigerians today seems to be that the leaders are above the law. People were forced to develop this opinion as a result of series of events and occasions in which the government or elected leaders disobeyed court orders. In each of these occasions, the court has been handicapped and unable to enforce compliance. The activities of most Nigerian leaders rubbish the ideal of the judiciary. This is so serious that most of the things we tell students about the power of the courts are fast becoming a mere academic exercise.

To place oneself above the law is not common to the serving leaders alone, even the ex-leaders do the same. Instances of showing lack of regard to the rule of law by past and present leaders shall be discussed. First to be discussed is the summoning of ex-military leaders General Ibrahim Babangida and General Muhammadu Buhari before Oputa Panel which they both refused to appear. Oputa Panel was set up by the civilian regime of Chief Olusegun Obadanjo to investigate past human right abuses that occurred under the military with the mandate of reconciling and rehabilitating the victims. These two ex-military leaders shunned the summons and refused to appear before the panel. Despite the fact that the panel was legally set up, nothing could be done to force them to appear before the panel. To most Nigerians, the actions of these two ex-leaders was not only uncivilized but tantamount to considering oneself to be above the law and showing lack of respect to the rule of law.

Another case was the one involving the Lagos State Government and the Federal Government. The Lagos State Government created new local governments which was constitutional and attested to by many people to have followed the procedure for creating new local governments.

The Federal Government under the leadership of Chief Olusegun Obasanjo ordered a reversal to the old number of 20 from the new 51 which the Lagos State Government under the leadership of Governor Bola Ahmed Tinubu refused to do. Consequent upon his refusal to revert to the old number of local governments, the Federal Government stopped allocation to all the Local Governments in Lagos State, both new and old ones. As a result of this stoppage of funds, the State Government went to the Supreme Court for clarification if the Federal Government had any power under the law to stop allocation of fund to any tier of government. The Supreme Court thus clarified that the Federal Government lack the jurisdiction to withhold fund meant for any tier of government. That the newly created local governments in Lagos State followed the laid down procedure though not yet finally ratified by the Federal legislators who owns the duty to give a final approval by amending the constitution and include the newly created councils. That the Federal Government should immediately release money meant for the local government to the 21 local governments pending the time the federal legislators will do their job by carrying out the necessary adjustment and absorb the newly created local government into the existing ones.

The Federal Government under the leadership of Chief Olusegun Obasanjo refused completely to obey the court order. Many months passed after the judgement, the Federal Government did not release the fund until the state reverted back to the old number of local governments.

The Federal government initially decided to seek clarification over the judgement which the court struck out because according to the court, the judgement was clear enough. The court could not do anything to force the President to obey the court order.

Another important contravention of the constitution that is worth mentioning here, was the arrest and detention of serving Governor of Anambra State Dr. Ngige by his political god father Chris Uba in connivance with the Nigerian Police. According to the Constitution of the Federal Republic of Nigeria (1999) the Governor is highly immunized against arrest and detention while in office. But this was contravened in 2003 when Governor Ngige of Anambra State was arrested by the Police and detained for almost a whole day under the auspices of his political god father Chris Uba. Uba did it and went scot free because of his wealth and secondly, he had powerful connection with the presidency. Ngige's arrest was not only a shock to Nigerians but the whole world. What Uba did and nothing happened, if somebody who is not properly connected tries it, he would die in jail. Apart from corruption, inequality before the law is another major problem facing the Nigerian democracy.

Some people seem to be above the law. The court suppose to be the last hope of common man, that is, one must be sure of justice when you go to court, but this was not always true in

Nigeria. Some judges in Nigerian courts are ready to tamper justice with money, not mercy as it is usually said. We have seen cases of misgiving of justice in the past, where judgement would be pronounced in favour of a guilty person because he had money.

It must be clearly stated here that the issue of lack of regard to the rule of law is not peculiar to the federal government alone. Some state governments are in the habit of disobeying court orders, perhaps because they appoint and promote the judges at the state level. The court cannot enforce order when Chief Executive disobeys it. There is no doubt that this is a bad signal for any democracy. There is no way democracy can succeed if the rule of law is not respected. It is the rule of law that greases and sustains democracy; it is the referee of the political game. When the rule of law is sidetracked, what we have has seized to be democracy but dictatorship.

African governments, though democratic in name they are far from being democratic in practice. That is why it is strongly believed that the problem of Nigeria is not the constitution but attitude. No matter how good a nation's constitution is, it will not implement itself. It is the people that will implement it. How effective and productive a constitution would be depends on how it is properly and genuinely implemented. Where people do contrary to the constitutional provisions, you cannot expect to get the constitutional desired results.

Nigerian democracy has not made strict observance, regard and adherence to the rule of law as its bedrock. People get to office and place themselves above the law that brought them in, there is inequality before the law, even though it is stated in the constitution that there is equality before the law, reverse is the case in practice as Nigerian laws respect the rich and powerful. Except all these abnormal situations are normalised, Nigerian democracy would be nothing more than a mere acquisition of power by the rich and utilization of power at the detriment of the poor masses.

One other problem with the system of justice in Nigeria is delayed justice. There is no efficiency and effectiveness in the way justice are dispensed in Nigeria. A case may drag for two or more years before judgement. People associate courts proceeding with come today come tomorrow. A lot of people are not ready to take their cases to court because they feel that not only would it waste their time but at the end justice may elude them. Suspects are remanded in prison custody for years in some cases without judgement. Some are forgotten in prison without judgement. Some who would have spent six months in prison end up spending three years without judgement. A person who was detained for three years for an offence which carries six months imprisonment on conviction has suffered more than required and no form of compensation for such people

Democracy is supposed to change this ugly situation but it has not done so. The irony of it is that President Chief Olusegun Obasanjo who was at a time an inmate who was expected to use his office to effect a change had not done anything in this regard. Nigerian prisons are highly dehumanized, no good food, no good treatment when they are sick, no neat environment for them to live in and even a domestic animal is of higher value in the hands of its owners than the prisoner in the hands of Nigerian government. An offender must be punished but not necessarily to take his life for a minor offence especially when he had not killed. The essence of punishing people should be to serve as a deterrent to other people, to reform the offender and to reattribute him to the society.

In conclusion, Nigerian democracy needs to embark on total reformation of the judicial system and develop the faith of Nigerians in the judiciary by ensuring equality of every citizen before the law, total regard for the rule of law and by making the judiciary to be completely independent of the other two arms of government as entrenched in the constitution. Except a strong judicial system that is independent, unprejudiced, unbiased, effective and efficient are put in place, democracy would not be firmly rooted.

Nigerian Democracy and Political Conflict

Attempt shall be made under this sub-heading to conceptualized conflict and highlight causes of conflict in Nigerian democracy vis-a-vis ways by which we can guide against political conflict in Nigeria.

Conflict according to Asoga-Allen (2004) can be defined as a state of disagreement between people, groups, countries and so on and so forth. It may also mean fighting or a war. Whenever two or more individuals or groups come into contact with each other, they may choose to make their relationship primarily conflictual or integrative (i.e. cooperative, supportive, agreed upon). If the initial relationship is primarily conflicted, there will nevertheless emerge at least a few minimal strands of misunderstanding and reciprocity rules of combat or perhaps only an agreement to disagree. If on the other hand, the initial relationship is primarily integrative, it is certain that conflict will develop, if for no other reason than through the demands of the association itself as they compare with the preferences of individual and component groups.

According to Bernard (1957), there is some degree of community organisations or integration in the concept of conflict. If the parties in question were not in the same place at the time or performing two incompatible functions at the same time, or cooperating to inflict reciprocal injury, there would be no conflict. Conflict may result in the disruption or destruction of all or certain of the bonds of unity that may previously have existed between the disputants.

Conflict takes place between two individuals, between individual and organisations or groups, between an organisation and one or more of its component parts of a single organisation or group. A conflict emerges whenever two or more persons (or groups) seek to possess the same object occupying the same space or the same exclusive position, play incompatible roles, maintain incompatible goals or undertake mutually incompatible means for achieving their purposes.

The above discussion on conflict is relevant to political conflict. It occurs whenever two or more persons (or groups) seek to possess the same exclusive position, occupying the same seat or space or undertake mutually incompatible means for achieving their purposes. Ideally, conflicts in democracy are not an aberration as observed by Asoga-Allen (2004). It is a visual phenomenon especially with a young democracy that is just springing out roots. Human beings being what we are, find it difficult to accept defeat. It takes high level of self development and maturity for one to attain that level of maturity.

Another important fact is that when two persons or groups are both struggling for a thing of value, it is basic that one person or group would finally have it that would lead to the emergence of a winner and a looser. In most cases, the looser whether with evidence or without evidence would jump into a conclusion that the winner had ran fowl the rules of the game. It is innate of every human being to find excuses to a situation of defeat. At the school level, when a student fails an internal examination, he would tell you. It is because the teacher/lecturer hates him, a female student may say that, it is because the teacher/lecturer made love proposal to her and she refused. Though, there are situations where this might be true, but in most cases it is a mere self defence to cover up inadequacies.

At the level of politics it is the same story. The party who lost an election would always see the part that won to have rigged the election. That is not to say that rigging of election is impossible. There are desperate politicians who are ready to do anything just to emerge victorious in an election. In essence, whether there is foul play or not there is bound to be a conflictual situation, when two persons or groups compete for something of value and honour and one person or group eventually emerges a winner. However, it is pertinent to say that the difference between genuine claim and in-genuine claim or accusation is the magnitude of the conflict. When one is accusing another falsely, he knows within himself, even if others do not know, and the level and vigour with which one would pursue false claim may not be the same with those of true claim.

It is usually for the looser to always find fault against the winner. In this perspective, the looser may accept defeat reluctantly without saying a word and later start to find faults against the winner, may be from the way he goes about his administration. If that is done so frequently, it would result in conflict. Also, there are instances where the winner would now want to use his power and influence to terrorise his opponent. Not necessarily a winner alone, where a contestant in an election is still in power as a president or governor. There is no way there would be the same level ground for all the contestants. The tendency for the one who is still in power to influence his re-election is very high. Such situation is not only abnormal but prone to injustice, political victimization and terrorism. It can prevent credible people from coming out to contest an election because they would not want to risk their lives.

Causes of Conflict in Democracy

Asoga-Allen (2004) highlighted eleven causes of conflict in democracy, these are:

1.   Unequal opportunity
2.   Rigging of election
3.   Bad leadership
4.   Poverty
5.   Unpopular government policies
6.   Political immaturity
7.   Religious intolerance
8.   Monopoly of power by one ethnic group
9.   Inter-ethnic struggle
10.   Unemployment, and
11.   Corruption

1.   **Unequal opportunity**: This is a situation whereby some citizens are ranked above the other or are considered to be more important than the other in terms of opportunities and benefits accruing to the citizens in the state. For example, where only the children of the rich are considered for important positions in the civil service or in politics, is very dangerous. In democracy,

people are expected to be equal, regardless of the socio-economic status or wealth or the political party individual belongs to or the tribe they come from. Where reverse is the case, conflict is bound to occur.

2.   **Rigging of election**: In democracy, those to represent the people are picked through election. Ideally, an election of such nature needs to be free and fair. That is, represent the will of the people. Where this is conspicuously rigged in favour of a particular candidate or political party, conflict would occur.

3.   **Bad leadership**: This is another major cause of conflict in democracy. A leader is expected to rule by the constitution and display high sense of responsibility, patriotism, accountability and probity. In like manner, a leader is expected to love his nation than he loves himself by embarking on people oriented programmes, not programmes that would benefit only the rich or few privilege individuals in the society. Where a leader pursues policies that make life difficult and hard for the people he governs and gives himself to acquisition of wealth while others suffer and lavish in the bondage of poverty, conflicts are bounds to occur.

4.   **Poverty**: This is another usual cause of conflict in democracy. Poverty is a condition of not being able to meet the essential needs of life especially the basic needs which include food, shelter and clothing. Where a man is not able to meet these three basic needs, his emotion and thinking becomes negative rather than

positive. He becomes aggressive over trivial issues. When majority of the people are in this state, conflicts are bound to happen.

5.   **Unpopular government policies**: This is another cause of conflict in democracy. Any government policy that affects the lives of the masses negatively or too harsh for the people to bear may result in conflict. Government owes it a duty to consider the interest of the people when taking any policy. Failure to do this sometimes may be disastrous.

6.   **Political immaturity**: This also causes conflict in democracy. Politics as an act need to be practised with maturity. Politics should not be a do or die affair. There is bound to be multi-party system and the people have the freedom to choose a party of their choice without molestation from the opposition party. Also when people contest for an elective position, it is certain that a winner must emerge at the end of the competition. Where people are not mature enough to respect the rights of others, and where a looser in an election is not mature enough to accept defeat in good faith or take the right step of seeking redress on account of election malpractices, conflicts are bound to occur.

7.   **Religious intolerance**: This is another likely cause of conflict in democracy. Religion is the belief in Supreme Being. It is something that is supposed to be between man and his God. It is not, and should not be an issue

to be forced on another person. In the real sense of it, only God knows who is a religious man because God looks at the inward while man looks at the outward. To distinguish oneself or making one particular pattern of dress for one self or spare hairs or beards does not mean that the person is religious, all these are outward things. However, if one is full of virtues and follows the doctrines which God requires man to follow in a particular religion; one may say that the person is religious. It is now left for God to judge whether it is true that the man is Godly or not. To force man against his belief is not only inhuman but barbaric and oppressive. You can only convince people to accept your religion through your behaviour not through the use of force. Where force is used, the action is far from being Godly but devilish and fanatic. Where people try to score political goal through religion may lead to conflict. More especially where one tend to portray his religion as superior to the other religions.

8. **Monopoly of power by one ethnic group**: This is also capable of causing conflict. In any country where there are multi-ethnic groups, the political arrangements suppose to give opportunity for all. That is, every ethnic group should be capable of producing the president. Not that one ethnic group would see the position of president as its legacy and that other tribes should not aim at it. Where this is the order of the day, marginalisation resulting from such action would result

into conflict

9. **Inter-ethnic struggle**: Ideally in a democracy, every ethnic group is supposed to be equal, where an ethnic group or tribe feels that he is superior to other ethnic groups, political conflicts are bound to happen. As observed by Asoga-Allen (2004) where one ethnic group claims to be superior to the others or deprive the others of importance, recognition, power, influence to mention a few, conflict would occur.

10. **Unemployment**: This is another cause of conflict. It is a serious social evil in every human society. A jobless man is a deprived man with less recognition and importance in the society. It is a deprivation that is capable of causing the deprived to use his potential negatively as a result of frustration that likely accompanies it. There is tendency for a frustrated man to join bad gangs or ethnic militia who are ready to commit illegality in the name of defending their people. Where unemployment is so rampant and the number of unemployed seems greater than those that are employed the economy would suffer depression. The resultant effect of this whether sooner or later is conflict.

11. **Corruption**: This may be defined as illegal acquisition of wealth or confiscating what belongs to the majority into one's use. It can also be defined as an act that is against the law or norms, values and general acceptance of the people. Any nation where corruption

is a way of life, there would rarely be equitable distribution of resources. Instead, everybody would be talking of self and be struggling for self, and thereby becoming self-centred. In such a country, those entrusted with the national resources use to take more than their actual shares of the national resources thereby putting the majority in abject poverty and penury. A situation where people always steal from an economy to bank it in another economy as it is the case with most African countries portrays a dangerous signal to the African economy and development. This would certainly lead to crises, especially when the tolerance of the masses has reached a climax or saturated level (Asoga-Allen, 2003). In the light of the above, people suffering in bondage of poverty would react negatively over trivial issues and engage each other in a duel over insignificant issues. It is important to stress that the causes of conflict in Nigeria today are more of poverty, unemployment, ethnic superiority struggle, power struggle between politicians and religious fanaticism than other factors or reasons.

Resolving Conflicts through Citizenship Education

What is Citizenship Education? Citizenship Education has been defined by various scholars in various ways. The definition of each scholar arose from the perception of individual scholar of the concept. One important similarity in the definitions of the scholars is the fact that they all agreed that it is an education given by the state to her citizens to keep them conscious of their rights, and obligations to the state vis-a-vis to the responsibilities of the state to the people. The scholars who have attempted to conceptualise Citizenship Education include Ezegbe (1988)' who sees Citizenship Education as an education through which pupils in the school system will be taught about their rights, privileges, duties and responsibilities as good citizens and through which they will be encouraged to seek such rights and privileges, perform their duties and play a positive and active role in the society.

Osakwe and Itejere (1993) define Citizenship Education as the systematic process through which young people acquire or internalise the values, sentiments and norms of the society in which they live and actively get involved to ensure that the common goals of the society is catered for, including resisting anti-social and unguided "youthful exuberance". They explained that Citizenship Education involves critical thinking, political activism or inquiry plus the goals and values of a good citizen.

Coleman (1965) in his effort to define Citizenship Education sees the subject as political socialisation. According to him, it is the process by which individual acquire attitudes and feelings towards the political system and towards their roles in it. He outlines what the process involved as:

*   Learning how the political system works;

*   The growth of feelings (positive and negative) about the

system; and

*   Development or non development of a sense of competence to participate actively in politics

Asoga-Allen (2001) defines Citizenship Education as that education given by a state to its citizens to enable them to be conscious of their rights, duties, responsibilities and obligations in the society vis-a-vis the expected roles of the government to the people.

Niemeyer (1957) sees Citizenship Education as an education that helps children to be socially intelligent members of the community. Citizenship Education finds its best application in the social context and involves acquisition of knowledge, attitudes and skills which will be utilized for the overall benefit of the society (Nwanyanwu, 1977).

Ignorance is not an excuse in the law court. And an accused is presumed an innocent until his case has been proved beyond all reasonable doubt. Most of the people in prison today as observed by Asoga-Allen (2001) are there for an offence which they committed unintentionally that is, through contravention of certain portion of the law which they are ignorance of its existence. Most people behave the way they do because of ignorance of the law. In essence, not everybody would like to kill another person if they knew that if they kill, they too would be killed. Or if they assault another fellow overtly or covertly, they would be imprisoned if taken up in the law court.

Those who are conversant with judgements in the court of law or who go to witness court proceedings would agree that psychologically, there are differences between the way those who committed offence or broke the law deliberately and those who did the same out of ignorance, when judgements are pronounced against them in the law court. Those who knew the consequences of certain behaviour before they carried it out would seem not bothered no matter the punishment. A good example is that of armed robbers. They rarely bother when they are condemned even to death in the law court. But where one did not know the consequences of an action and was caught in that action and later condemned by the court of law, he feels bitter and shed tears.

Though this is not in all cases, one may shed crocodile tears whether he committed an offence deliberately or indeliberately. Acknowledgeable person easily knows the difference by watching with a keen interest the condemned person's expression of bitterness as a result of the sentence. That is the reason why the issue of enlightenment of the citizens should be taken serious by the government. Most governments; especially in African continent are guilty of high level of ignorance being suffered by their citizens. In most cases laws are made without the knowledge of the masses, one would get to know about the law only when one has contravened it and he is caught in the act.

Awareness of the law or constitution can be carried out by the government through radios, televisions, newspapers, signposts and handbills. The most effective way of doing this is through education in school. A course like Citizenship Education if properly taught has the potentials of producing enlightened citizens. Let us look at the objectives of Citizenship Education. Citizenship Education as a course in the curriculum of schools in Nigeria has the following objectives

a. To create the awareness of the Nigeria constitution and the need for democracy in Nigeria

b. To acquaint Nigerians with the functions and obligations of the government

c. To create adequate functional political literary among the people;

d. To make Nigerians fully conscious of their rights, duties and obligations and to respect the rights of others;

e. To assist in the production of responsible, well-informed and self-reliant Nigerian citizens;

f. To inculcate the right values e.g. honesty, integrity, hard work, faithfulness, fairness and justice. To foster attitudes of togetherness, comradeship and cooperation among the various peoples of Nigeria;

g. To inculcate the concept of authority, leadership and followership into the citizens;

h. To produce citizens who are capable of participating meaningfully in discussions on the Nigerian system of government and electoral process, arms of government, code of conduct for public officers and roles of mass media in national development;

i. To articulate our history, national symbols, people and cultures of Nigeria; and

j.   To discuss the characteristics features of the Nigerian environment as well as the roles of national and international conservation agencies.

One would agree with me that these are laudable objectives that are capable of transforming the country to a peaceful society where citizens know the law and abide by the law and struggle for the betterment of their country. One unique thing about Citizenship Education is that the experiences it impact are such that are needed by man throughout life. Citizenship Education remains with the individual learner for as long as he lives. No man is an island; man lives in the midst of others and in fact needs others. For him to live a peaceful life, a life that is free from oppression, violence, crime, ignorance and dogmatism, he needs the knowledge of Citizenship Education.

If students only study the course for examination purpose, that is, just to pass it in the examination, the objectives are far from being achieved. There must be practical evidence that the students have actually assimilated the values of the course. Asoga-Allen (2001) outlined ten qualities that must be imbibed and demonstrated by students or anyone who have passed through Citizenship Education. These qualities are:

a.   Consciousness of his rights and the rights of others;
b.   Being able to function effectively and efficiently in any governmental institutions;
c.   Possession and demonstration of political knowledge;
d.   Being loyal and patriotic;
e.   Putting national interest above self interest;

f.   Being highly disciplined;

g.   Interacting freely with the various ethnic groups in the country;

h.   Respecting the constitutions of the Federal Republic of Nigeria;

i.   Being nationalistic in approach rather than tribalistic; and

j.   Making accountability and probity their watchword in both private and public lives.

At this juncture, it is obvious that Citizenship Education remains an indispensable instrument for conflict resolution in every society. To make this workable and practicable, a lot of efforts and resources need to be put in place and tailored towards the enlightenment of the citizens. It is a basic fact that most of the Nigerian citizens today are not enlightened. That is why anti-social behaviours, crimes, and criminalities are so rampant. A lot of government officers are ignorant of the functioning of the government. Common national anthem, some public officers do not know. That shows the magnitude of ignorance in the country. The problem of lack of enlightenment on the part of the citizenry is not peculiar to Nigeria alone; the story is the same with most African nations.

The present content of the course in our schools needs to be reformed if the course is expected to achieve its objectives. The content does not include some essential facts that a child needs to know. To make the course serve the purpose of conflict prevention and resolution, the following should be done:

a. Citizenship Education should be properly taught from primary to the tertiary level and it should be made compulsory;

b. The content of the course should include what constitutes offences or regarded as offences in the country and the penalties for each of the offences. If this is done, people would think twice before they commit crime.

c. Knowledge of Citizenship Education should be a pre-requisite for electing people into public offices, those who lack knowledge of Citizenship Education, should not be elected;

d. Examples of court cases and judgement on some criminal offences should be brought to the knowledge of the students.

e. Teachers should be prepared specially to teach the course. And such teacher must be screened and be found to be of high moral standard, not someone who would say or preach something and do contrary to what they preach

f. Assessment of the course should not be based on written examination alone; it should be 50% examination and 50% practical. The students should be monitored and corrected when need be.

If all these are done, conflict would be prevented since conflict prevention is better than conflict resolution. The issue of ignorance would become a thing of the past. Those in politics would know that politics is not a do or die affair, that one looses to win and wins to lose. Citizenship Education would ensure accountability and probity in government. It would quench the spirit of self that is so rampant among African leaders. There would be good government, corruption would be wiped out. Equal opportunities for all citizens as entrenched in the constitution would be followed and made practicable. Injustice in the law court would become a thing of the past.

Equitable distribution of resources would bring about good employment opportunities for all citizens, unemployment related vices like armed robbery, advanced fee fraud known as 419, to mention a few, would become things of the past. One ethnic group would see another as equal and important and this would eliminate inter-tribal or inter-ethnic wars and conflict. All fraudulent activities associated with buying and selling in the market would be fenced out.

It is a basic fact that conflict cannot be completely wiped out of human society but with Citizenship Education, such conflict would not be violent and bloody. Resolution of such conflict would be easy because the disputants would know their limit. People would refrain from jungle justice when there is conflict, rather, they would prefer to seek redress in the appropriate court of law. There would be peaceful society with less number of conflicts to resolve.

In conclusion, if the high rate of conflicts in African nations must be reduced, prevented and resolved, Citizenship Education must be given a pride of place in the society. Citizens must be properly taught not only to know their rights but to claim their rights and perform their obligations to the government and on the part of the government, there should be good governance, equitable distribution of resources, fairness and equity in handling the affairs of the people. Openness, transparency, accountability and probity should be made a guiding principle.

CHAPTER FIVE: SOME PAST NIGERIAN LEADERS

Chief Obafemi Awolowo (Old Western Region)

If ability to ensure good condition of living for the masses by lifting them socially, morally, politically, economically and psychologically is an attribute of greatness, then, the reign of Chief Obafemi Awolowo deserves special political and historical attention. He was a distinguished politician who undoubtedly pursued the greatness of Nigeria by using education as an instrument of human investment and transformation. He was the premier of the old western region who devoted his full attention to all round development of the old western state of Nigeria

Economically, he was a great economist and a prudent manager of both human and material resources who made accountability and probity his watchword. He encouraged agriculture especially cocoa plantation, and this formed the major means of foreign exchange for the region. Old western region was one of the world leading producer of and exporter of cocoa during his tenure. Cocoa trade became so prosperous that multi-floor cocoa house was built in Ibadan, the capital of old western region. He put in place an effective tax system. Both men and women were made to pay general tax to the government purse. Income tax was also introduced for civil servants and business people. Proceeds from these taxes and export of cocoa were channelled towards developmental projects like education, health, building of industries, construction of roads and so on and so forth. Employment opportunities were created for the people both in public and private sector of the economy.

The economy of the region under his tenure was buoyant that a group of investments known as Oodua Investments sprang up. These included estate management, banks, manufacturing companies, printing press, to mention a few. Also important was the establishment of Western Nigerian Broadcasting Corporation (WNBC) which was said to be the first television station in West Africa.

Educationally, being a highly educated man, he cherished and embraced education as an instrument of liberating human mind from the bondage of ignorance and poverty. To this end, he introduced a successful Free Primary Education (FPE) in old Western Region. His FPE programme did not only carry free tuition but also included free text-books. A lot of people who were unable to afford the cost of education before were now able to go to school. That led to the emergence of new crop of educated elite. Millions of people in the old Western Region are educated today as a result of the opportunity provided by Chief Obafemi Awolowo. In fact, this free education opportunity explains why there is educational imbalance between the West and the North or East today. Schools were built, teacher training institutions were established and older ones were expanded to cope with training of teachers. Graduates of educational institutions were given immediate employment.

He laid a solid foundation for the old Western Region in terms of economic, social and politics. He contested an election to be president in the second republic but the election was manipulated in favour of his opponent. This was so because he had the majority of the votes cast in the election but the issue of 2/3 majority was used to rob him of his victory in the election. If he had been allowed to rule in the second republic as president, his economic agenda would have transformed the nation to one of the greatest country in the world.

It is pertinent to say that the economic woe and suffering which Nigerians are going through today was prophesized or foretold by Chief Obafemi Awolowo. The National Party of Nigeria (NPN) that won the election had a lot of things to borrow from the economic proposal of Awolowo but due to the calibre of people that dominated the party and their personal ambition to enrich self, they refused to have anything doing with his agenda. Even when he warned against the unscrupulous and fraudulent spending of the NPN government led by Alhaji Shehu Shagari, his warning was ignored and he was tagged a nuisance. At the end of it all what he said concerning the nation came to pass.

It is true that he is dead but history will not forget him as one of the greatest if not the greatest son of Oduduwa. His political, social, economic and administrative ingenuity are unprecedented in the history of Nigeria. He will be remembered by many generations for his contributions to human and national development.

Other premiers or his contemporaries at that time included Sir Abubakar Tafawa Balewa of the Northern Region, Akpabi Azikhia of the Mid-Western Region. Each of these people also contributed in one way or the other to the development of their people and the nation as a whole.

Major General Yakubu Gowon (1966 - 1975)

Gowon became the military head of state on July 1966 after a military coup that ousted General Aguyi Ironsi who reigned between January 1966 and July 1966. He was the youngest General that ever ruled Nigeria. During his tenure as military head of state, the economy of the nation was in right shape. His tenure did not only witness oil boom but the proceeds from the boom were appropriately utilized for developmental projects that is, projects that are capable of transforming the nation into one of the greatest and enviable nation in the world.

His period witnessed mass construction of roads, bridges in various parts of Nigeria. There were employment opportunities for Nigerians during his tenure.

During the period of Yakubu Gowon, the nation went into war against Colonel Odumegwu Ojukwu and the easterner generally when they attempted to break away from Nigeria in

1967, by declaring the bright of Biafra. The war lasted for almost three years and was won by the Nigerian soldiers. His ability to keep Nigeria one at that crucial period was a demonstration of military competence, courage and bravery.

During his time, little was heard about corruption that seems to have engulfed the nation today. Gowon ruled for almost nine years before he was overthrown in a military coup led by General Murtala Muhammed. Though, Yakubu Gowon ruled the nation as a military head of state which had no legal right to rule but one thing is important here this is his achievements as a ruler. Yakubu Gowon becomes eminent in the history of Nigeria not because he ruled the nation but by the fact that he was not a self-centred, corrupt and selfish leader. There was no form of accusation of corruption against General Yakubu Gowon and he did not accumulate wealth for himself as did by most of the leaders that came after him. His lifestyle and philosophy is worthy of emulation.

Alhaji Shehu Shagari (1979 - 1983)

Alhaji Shehu Shagari ascended the throne as President of the Federal Republic of Nigeria in the year 1979. He was declared the winner of the election which he contested with Chief Obafemi Awolowo after the issue of 2/3 majority was manipulated in his favour. His immediate predecessor was Chief Olusegun Obasanjo who ruled the nation as military head of state between 1976 and 1979. Alhaji Shehu Shagari inherited a sound economy from General Olusegun Obasanjo.

A huge sum of about Eight billion Naira was handed over by Obasanjo administration to Shagari. No sooner Shagari ascended the throne than he lavished the nation's resources and ran the economy bankrupt.

In the first place, no one expected that the calibre of person that the whole north would present for the post of president could be as low as Shagari then. The problem faced by Shagari during his administration was more of incompetence than that of bad companies. The situation looked as if those who brought Shagari out did so with the aim of manipulating or using him to share the national resources. In essence, he was picked perhaps, those who picked him saw him as an easy instrument that could be used to achieve selfish goal.

Economically, within first year of his administration, the economy of the nation was already bastardized, the treasury was looted, income from the crude oil and other sources were unaccounted for and diverted to private uses. Before the third year of his administration, the nation was already in serious debt. Foreign loans were obtained without anything to show for it. There was open display of wealth by many political office holders as they became stinking rich, as a result of corruption perpetrated by them. At least about five ministers were having private jets in addition to chain of expensive cars which they packed in their mansions.

Civil servants, especially the teachers were ploughed into poverty and starvation as their salaries were not paid for months. In some states teachers' salaries were paid not more than four times in a year. This situation forced many teachers into petty trading and their attentions were thus divided which has serious implications for education of the nation. The general public was not left out of the untold suffering which corrupt administration of Shehu Shagari brought upon the people

It must be stressed that part of the debt that the nation paid the group of eight highly industrialised nations (G8) and Paris Club were incurred during Shagari's administration. Contracts were awarded and payment made in full without any work done at the site of the contract, contract fees were inflated to favour the awarder and the awardee.

Politically, the system of government operated by Shehu Shagari cannot be regarded as democracy; rather it would be more appropriate to describe his regime as autocratic. This is true to a large extent that people were robbed of one vital aspect of their fundamental human rights which is the freedom of expression. People were not allowed to express their opinion during Shagari's regime. To buttress this point, a lot of people were recruited into National Security Organization (NSO) then which is known today as State Security Service. A lot of people were arrested and detained because they expressed themselves about the nation. It is believed that the number of NSO then would be far greater than that of the police; this was because they were found almost everywhere. Even in the bus of mass transit vehicle locally called molue, they were represented. When you say your opinion on any national issue that seems uncomplimentary to the president or those in government, the person would be arrested as he steps out of the bus and be taken away.

The relationship between the Executive and Legislature was so smooth or cordial because they were partners with the same criminal objective to loot the treasury and become billionaires. The rate at which the treasury was looted during Shagari's regime was unprecedented in the history of Nigeria. No wonder, when the government was toppled in 1983, many top officials in the government ran into exile e.g. Umaru Dikko who was a Minister in the regime. If Nigerians are not so forgetful, they will never forget the hardship they went through during Shehu Shagari's regime.

Economically, the nation could not be said to have any plan or destination during Shagari's reign. In essence, there was no meaningful economic agenda. The only plan that could be identified or recognized at this material time was the plan to spend without minding the income. Income from crude oil was wasted without thinking about the future of the nation and her people. As a result of reckless spending embarked upon by the government, internal and external debt piled up. The nation could no longer meet her financial commitments and it had to go borrowing. The economic depression that accompanied looting of the nation's treasury was so great that many Nigerian students on scholarship abroad were withdrawn from their various institutions because of government inability to fulfil her obligations to their institutions.

It is not an exaggeration to say that Shagari's administration brought great set back to the economic, political and social life of Nigerians. In many states, education suffer serious setback. Apart from the dilapidated and obsolete infrastructure, the teachers' salaries and allowances were not paid for years. This culminated into teachers' strike for months. Where there was no strike, teacher came to work when they like since they were not paid, they had to look for extra job to feed themselves and their families.

To most Nigerians then, the intervention of the military to overthrow Shagari's regime was timely and inevitable because the regime was already in a state of confusion and the business of governance was already grounded due to corruption, self-centredness, indiscipline, incompetence and handling of the nation's affairs by bloody rogues.

If Nigeria had been a civilized country like America, Britain etc, people like Shagari and those who served in his regime would have been made to apologise to Nigerians for the hardship which they pushed the people into during their regime. Also it is doubtful if people like Shehu Shagari and some looters who ruled Nigeria in the past that are being recognised today as patriots really deserve the honour being given to them. It is commonsensical that it is not to become president that matters but what you achieved during your tenure. A ruler or leader that reigns and things were alright with the people would not be forgotten and the ruler or leader that reigns and people were eating sand when they cannot afford good food would also be remembered. But the difference is the type of remembrance. While one would be remembered as a good ruler or leader, the other would be regarded as evil and bad leader. A good leader and a bad leader cannot be said to deserve the same honour.

In conclusion, not all the past leaders that the nation is floating today as patriots deserve that honour. Some of them are a curse to the nation and the wound which they inflicted on the nation and her people will remain indelible in the minds of those who witnessed it. If they are still drawing any benefit from the nation on the ground of being past leaders, it is a shortage to the nation. Rather, most of them are expected to be made to give account of their stewardship and also be asked to pay the nation back the money that they embezzled. It is only by doing this that leadership can be meaningful and people-oriented in Nigeria.

General Ibrahim Gbadamosi Babangida (1985 - 1993)

He came to the throne of leadership of the Federal Republic of Nigeria after a coup that ousted Generals Muhammed Buhari/Idiagbon's regime. General Muhammed Buhari/Idiagbon was overthroned at a time when it was trying to wash Nigeria and Nigerians of moral decadence and large magnitude of indiscipline that characterised the nation. Orderliness was gradually being restored when Babangida and his men seized power from them. Babangida ruled the nation for eight years without anything to show for it in terms of social, political and economic development.

Economically, Babangida's period witnessed tremendous improvement in the sales of crude oil and revenue for the nation. His period witnessed Gulf War in which Nigeria realised more than twelve billion dollars in excess of the normal budget for a particular year. The irony of this huge revenue is that the money was embezzled as Babangida and his men cannot account for how the money was spent. Instead of encouraging economic growth and national development, Babangida's regime was bedevilled with unprecedented large scale corruption and indiscipline. Indiscipline reached the climax during the Babangida's regime. Corruption was legitimized. Advanced fee fraud known as 419 was practised at its highest level. Nigerians were seen as fraudulent people that were very dangerous to be trusted by the foreign nations.

The nation's gross domestic products increased vis-a-vis the national revenue but this did not translate into increase in the per capita income, neither did it result into economic growth as people languished in the cell of poverty and penury. Civil servants were poorly paid that many honest ones found it difficult to change their shoes let alone meeting the needs of their families. As a university graduate, your salary was about two thousand three hundred or four hundred depending on the entry step. Only just very few people who were closed to the corridor of power were able to make ends meet.

General Babangida was given all sorts of names by Nigerians because of his corrupt and cunning forwardness. For example, people called him Maradona, chop I chop, fifty-fifty and so on and so forth. When he embarked on any harsh economic policy and people cry foul, he would give them a peanut to pacify them. He pursued various economic measures such as Structural Adjustment Programme (SAP) devaluation of currency, austerity measure and so on and so forth which only paved way for his administration to have enough to loot from the nation's treasury. Despite the revenue or income of this regime, he obtained loans from the foreign nations. According to speculations from the government quarters, this loan was used for importing sardines for the armed forces and the Para-military organisations.

The Oputa Panel that investigated Babangida on the disappearance of 12 billion dollars realised from the sale of crude oil during the Gulf War indicted him of wasteful spending and corrupt practices. It is the belief of most Nigerians as at today that Ibrahim Babangida is richer than Nigeria as a nation. That what he stole from the nation's treasury spelled economic doom for the nation which would take years of economic resuscitation and reconstruction to recover from.

Politically, he was politically over ambitious, after ruling the nation for a period of eight years, he attempted to succeed himself. He organized an election in 1993 which was adjudged the most free and fair in the political history of Nigeria and the election was claimed to have been won by Chief M. K. O. Abiola who was an intimate friend of Babangida before the election. General Babangida annulled the election instead of handing over to Chief Abiola. The annulment of this election did not come as a surprise to Nigerians both at home and abroad only, but also to the international communities. It was after the annulment of the election that it became obvious that Babangida was not ready to relinquish power that his intention was to become life president. One major surprise to most Nigerians about the type of person Babangida was the fact that Chief Abiola claimed he consulted Babangida, his friend before coming out to contest the election and Babangida pledged his loyalty to Abiola and promised to support him. This unruly attitude of Babangida was resisted by Nigerians especially those from southern part of the country. Various organisations were formed to see out the then unpopular government of Babangida. Notable among the organisation was the National Democratic Coalition (NADECO). NADECO did not carry arms against the government of Babangida but engaged the government in intellectual warfare. The government was disregarded internationally and those serving in the government were not recognised internationally, especially United States and United Kingdom. Embargoes were placed on Nigeria by United

Nations, that no nation should sell military wares to Nigeria. In fact, Nigerian top government officers were banned from entering United States of America and United Kingdom. Also Nigeria was suspended from major international organisation like Common Wealth of Nations.

When Babangida discovered that there was no means for him to actualise his political ambition, he decided to step aside believing to come back at a later date. In fact, it took the efforts of the whole world to force out Babangida from power.

The way the Yoruba people handled the issue of annulment of June 12 presidential election is worthy of emulation by other tribes in Nigeria and even Africa. This was because the annulment was enough to cause another civil war if it were to be other tribes. And civil war would have caused the nation too much destruction which would affect African continent. This was so because the polity at that time was over-heated. The belief of northerners as at that time was that ruling Nigeria was their legacy, that other tribes were unfit to rule Nigeria. What that entails was that if you were not a northerner, you were a second rated citizen. The history of the past rulers of Nigeria tended to justify this erroneous and criminally inclined idea. Most of the past rulers of the country came from the north even though their reigns witnessed economic depression and stagnation which brought untold suffering on the masses. Instead of carrying arms to destroy the nation, people adopted intellectual warfare methods. Media houses and newspapers were used to cripple the government and the junta was forced out of power.

During Babangida's period, many ways of killing people came to be known e.g. through letter bomb, through injection and so on and so forth. One major event that Nigerians of that time cannot forget easily was the killing of Dele Giwa the publisher of News watch magazine with letter bomb. His friend who was with him when the letter was given to him, said that immediately the letter was handed over to Dele by the person who brought the letter, that Dele Giwa remarked that this must be a letter from Mr. President. In an attempt to open the letter, it exploded and killed him.

According to some Nigerians who alleged Babangida to have killed him claimed that Babangida killed him because a secret was about to be leaked by Dele Giwa. The secret was that a woman who was condemned to death for carrying drug (Mrs. Gloria Okon) and the government claimed they have executed by firing squard was found by Dele Giwa in London. When he returned to Nigeria, he was about circulating this through his newspaper, but before this came out, Gloria Okon was said to have telephoned Babangida that the secret was already out because Dele Giwa saw her in London. That Babangida moved immediately and terminated Dele Giwa's life to prevent the news that was capable of shaking the entire country from being published. The truth of the matter is yet to be established up till today.

According to Ribadu (2000) the regime of Shehu Shagari and Babangida were the most corrupt in the history of Nigeria, but to the surprise of most Nigerians these regimes were never probed. Only Abacha's regime received the attention of the Federal Government, perhaps because Abacha died on the throne. People believe that if Abacha were to be alive till today, he would have gone scot free with all the embezzled money.

Militarily, Babangida contributed nothing to the development of the Armed Forces which he came from. He met weak armed forces with outdated weapons and left the military with extremely weak and outdated weapons. The major task of Babangida was what to benefit from Nigeria; he had no interest in the development of Nigeria. He left Nigeria worst than he met it, still somebody like Babangida who impoverished the country and the people is still being paraded as past a leader of Nigeria, and member of the Council of State.

General Sanni Abacha Mohammed (1993 - 1998)

He was one of the worst leaders that ruled Nigeria. Abacha was not only corrupt but he was very wicked, unscrupulous, fetish and a sadistic. He came to the throne after he staged a coup that ousted Chief Earnest Shonekan who was the head of Babangida set-up interim government. He was an accomplice of Babangida's annulment of June 12 election believed to have been won by Chief Moshood Kashimawo Olawale Abiola. He was a defence minister under Babangida's regime, but instead of defending Nigeria, his father land, he was busy defending his pocket by converting all the money allocated for defence into his pocket.

Politically, Abacha ascended the throne at a time when the annulment of June 12 election had generated a lot of heat. People expected Abacha to redress the injustice by handing over power to Chief Abiola but Abacha who had been aspiring for the position of head of state for many years by participating in various coups, refused to hand over power. Instead, he clamped down on Abiola by ordering his arrest after he (Abiola) declared himself as the President of the Federal Republic of Nigeria. He ensured that Abiola was detained for years to enable him achieve his ambition of corruptly enriching himself

Abacha did not stop with the arrest and detention of Abiola, he clamped down on all the apostles of June 12. Anyone who was in support of actualisation of June 12 became Abacha's enemy. The method of using media houses and newspapers to campaign for the actualisation of June 12 during General Babangida's period was used during Abacha. The method forced Babangida out of power but Abacha remained unshaken. Abacha established killer squad headed by a major in the army, by name Al-Mustapha. This squad was responsible for the assassination of Kudirat Abiola, the wife of Chief M. K. O. Abiola. Many Nigerians were brutalised by the killer squad. Attempts were made by the killer's squad on the lives of many Nigerians who were anti-Abacha and pro-Abiola. These included Chief Ibru, Chief Gani Fawehinmi, Chief

Enahoro to mention a few. Many members of NADECO had to go on exile to avoid being killed. While on exile they continued to wage intellectual warfare against Abacha and his nepotic and callous government. Radio Kudirat was established abroad and was broadcasting to Nigeria and some parts of the world. People like Prof. Wole Soyinka were on exile and were a major general in the anti-Abacha's struggle. Abacha just like Babangida planned to establish his hegemony as life president by putting in motion all the needed machineries. He set up a committee to draft a new constitution for the country. The constitution was drafted in favour of Abacha and in such a way that would make him to have unlimited power. The transition government masterminded by Abacha's regime was designed to achieve the emergence of Abacha as the consensus president. Nobody was ready to contest with Abacha for presidency because everybody was protecting his head from danger. When Abacha discovered that Yoruba people were against his self succession bid, he framed up top Yoruba people in the Army and those who had retired from the Army that they planned to overthrow his government. General Olusegun Obasanjo, a former head of state and an elder statesman was arrested and accused of participating in a coup which people doubted its authenticity. Also arrested for coup attempt or framed in a coup plot was Lieutenant Oladipupo Diya, Abacha's second in command, General Adisa and some others who are top Yoruba people in the army. A military tribunal was set up to try them and they were sentenced to death by the tribunal.

In fact, General Sanni Abacha was desperate to wipe off the Yoruba race to enable him achieve his political ambition. Some few Nigerians who were from other tribes who spoke against Abacha self succession were arrested. Attempts were made on their lives by Abacha's agent through food poisoning, injection or killer fluid. One major person that fell victim of this was General Yar adua who was a second in command to Obasanjo during his tenure as military head of state. Yar-adua died in prison. According to speculation, he was injected with killer fluid. It took the special intervention of the Almighty God to save the other political detainees from the hands of Abacha. According to speculations there was already a plan to kill them at a scheduled date, but before the date fixed, God removed Abacha from existence. General Olusegun Obasanjo who had been condemned to death by Abacha was set free and succeeded in the transition election which Abacha planned but did not witness as president.

Economically, the five-year period that Abacha ruled Nigeria was a colossal waste to the country economically. There was no meaningful economic plan, no meaningful project was executed. Nigerians suffered like slave in their father land. People slept at the petrol station before they could get petrol to buy. Fuel is being sold at exorbitant rates. Income from crude oil was packed in foreign banks. Not only that Abacha was busy committing fraud but all members of his family were collecting money from the central bank, executing contracts, running Nigeria like a family business. Many Nigerians found it difficult to feed two times a day. Many parents could not provide good food for their children. Many children died of Kwashiorkor, a disease caused by lack of balanced diet. Workers were poorly paid; their take home pay could not take them anywhere. As a result of the chronic poverty that was ravaging the country; the level of intolerance was very high. People engaged themselves in a duel over trivial issues that could have been solved amicably. Armed robbery was so rampant everywhere. One could not sleep and close his two eyes in the cities. Travellers especially by road and water were prone to attack by armed robbers. The defence of the country was not given a priority as the armed forces were left with obsolete weapons. At the level of internal security, the police force was poorly financed. No vehicles, no communication gadgets to fight crimes. The situation was so bad that policemen even the rank and file were to buy their official uniforms themselves. There was no form of incentives to the police.

Educationally, most of the nation's universities at Abacha's period became glorious secondary schools. No teaching facilities, modern laboratory equipments were in short supply, no allocation of fund to finance researches, no fund to maintain the old structures. The lecturers were not encouraged to carry out researches. Most of them found it difficult to meet the needs of their families and they had to look beyond the university community to make ends meet. There was a strike embarked upon by the university lecturers and non academic staff of universities that lasted for six months. When the strike was later called off, Abacha claimed that he did not know that the university lecturers were on strike. If the university lecturers could go through such ordeal, one can imagine what the teachers at the lower levels would be subjected to.

Education is usually the sector that suffers most as a result of any bad government in Nigeria. This is because most rulers of the country have more than enough for themselves and their generations yet unborn. They can afford to send their children to the most expensive universities in the world. In fact, you rarely see a child of top political office holder in public institutions. To many of them, they only pay lip service to funding education. Some see investment on education as a waste as this seems to reduce the money available for their private pockets. Some claimed that teachers are too many and retrenched teachers in their schools.

It is a clear fact, that Abacha was not the only treasury looter. It is believed by most Nigerians that Abacha did not steal as much as Babangida but one thing is that Abacha was a heartless human being, who though existed during the modern time but exhibited ancient, crude, archaic and uncivilized behaviour. The name Abacha was equated with cruelty, animosity, chaos and oppression. After the death of Abacha, millions of dollar were recovered from his foreign bank accounts e.g. Swiss bank, Switzerland bank and a host of others. As at the time this book was being written, some countries of the world are yet to assist Nigeria in recovering the looted money deposited in their banks by late Abacha.

Religiously, Abacha was such a person that believed that God could support evil doers once he had the money to hire sorcerer, diviner, powerful Alfas who offer sacrifices on a daily basis to God. According to speculations at the time of his death, Abacha harboured a lot of Alfas from various parts of the world who offered prayers for him on a daily basis and pleaded with God to support Abacha to fulfil his ambition to be life president, regardless of his behaviour. He claimed to belong to a religious sect but his behaviour was worse than that of a pagan or an atheist. One is not being sentimental by saying that the rulers from the northern part of Nigeria were the instruments used by the devil to impoverish the nation and her people because apart from General Yakubu Gowon, no meaningful development could be traced or associated with the other rulers from the north, their reigns brought the nation backwards rather than moving it forward. No wonder Abacha died a shameful death and Nigerians jubilated over his death. Abacha's death was seen by most Nigerians as a divine intervention to liberate Nigerians from the house of bondage and oppression. And people celebrated his death and rejoiced openly for God's salvation which He manifested for his people.

General Olusegun Obasanjo (1976 - 1979)

General Olusegun Obasanjo ascended the throne as the military Head of State after a bloody coup that ousted General

Muritala Ramat Mohammed in February 13, 1976. He was the second in command to General Muritala Mohammed. The sudden death of General Muritala Mohammed catapulted General Olusegun Obasanjo to the throne as the Military Head of State.

The economic policy pursued by General Olusegun Obasanjo though, brought hardship to the people but led to economic development. He was noted for strict economic policies. He ensured that money was not spent anyhow. During his first regime as military head of state, he encouraged agriculture. He was the one that introduced Operation Feed the Nation of the 1970s which made it mandatory for everyone to farm. To remove the bottleneck posed by land ownership problem, he enacted a decree which transferred the ownership of land to the Federal Government. With this decree, government has the right to acquire any land and use it for developmental project.

During his tenure as military Head of State, education was not well funded. There was crisis in the education sector which sparked off a mass protest popularly known as Ali must go by the Nigerian students. In essence, education was not properly funded during his first tenure.

Politically, he conducted a successful transitional election that brought in a democratically elected president in 1979. This successful transition earned him great international reputation. This was because he did not behave like most ex-military heads of state that preferred to remain in power for ever. Voluntarily without pressure, he handed over power. People considered this as a rare quality in him. Perhaps, this was the reason why the northern oligarchy had to bring him forward when the need arose to feature a Yoruba man as President of the Federal Republic of Nigeria. This could be supported with the fact that Chief Obasanjo handed over to a northerner (Alhaji Shehu Shagari) in 1979. Thus, the north saw him as their loyalist and a politically trustworthy person.

One quality in Chief Olusegun Obasanjo was that he is not wasteful. He does not encourage wastefulness. This explains why his regime witnessed accumulation of wealth for the nation. He handed over about eight billion naira to Alhaji Shehu Shagari in 1979. And that was when Nigerian naira was very powerful in the international market. To most Nigerians especially the Yoruba people, Obasanjo was too strict, wicked and stingy. To them, Obasanjo was such that does not believe in using his position to assist his people. Throughout his tenure as a military head of state, there was nothing to show for it in Yoruba land. Unlike his counterparts from the northern part of Nigeria who transformed their communities to small London by vantage of their positions. Obasanjo find it easier to help people from other tribes or embark on developmental projects in their territory than in the territory of his people.

He handed over power in 1979 to Alhaji Shehu Shagari and retired from the military into farming.

General Olusegun Obasanjo (1999 - 2007)

The second ascendance of Chief Olusegun Obasanjo to the humble throne of president of the Federal Republic of Nigeria was a miracle. Obasanjo never thought of becoming a president after he had retired from the army but whatever God packages as man's destiny must be fulfilled or certainly come to past. Chief Olusegun Obasanjo was already condemned to death over a coup which he was framed to have participated in. General Sanni Abacha whose ambition was to become life president implicated Chief Olusegun Obasanjo and other Yoruba top officers in the military. The major ambition of Abacha was to eliminate top Yoruba leaders in the military because he felt threatened by their continuous clamouring for the actualisation of June 12. To Abacha actualisation of June 12 would hamper his ambition to transform to a civilian president.

With the intervention of Nigerians and international communities, Obasanjo's death sentence was commuted to imprisonment. When Abacha died suddenly, the northerners realised that the only way to douse tension and heal the wound already inflicted on Yoruba people by the annulment of June 12 was to allow a Yoruba man to serve as president. This was what led to Obasanjo who was granted national pardon after the death of Abacha being called to become the presidential candidate under the Peoples Democratic Party (PDP). Eventually, he contested the election and won, and was sworn in as president of the Federal Republic of Nigeria and Commander in Chief of the Armed Forces.

The first step undertaken by Chief Olusegun Obasanjo was the touring of the world by visiting almost all countries of the world. The political aims of Obasanjo for undertaking this tour included:

1. To create a new image for Nigeria as a result of the already battered image created by the tyrant who ruled the country in the past.

2. To familiarise himself with the various world leaders by creating a good rapport between Nigeria and the various countries.

3. To convince the world leaders that Nigeria was not as bad as portrayed by the foreign media.

4. To attract international sympathy towards Nigeria so as to have her foreign debts cancelled

5. To secure foreign military backing towards enthroning an enduring and stable democracy in Nigeria.

6. To attract foreign investors to Nigeria.

7. For personal aggrandizement

Initially, Obasanjo was criticised by many Nigerians for wasting the national resources on travelling every time from one country to another. He was told several times to sit at home and solve his internal problems rather than going about. His gospel of debt forgiveness was seen by most Nigerians as an ambition that could not be fulfilled. This touring of the world that was criticised sooner or later started to yield good fruits for the country. The image of Nigeria changed for better in the international community, foreign investors from US, UK, Asia to mention a few started to visit Nigeria to access the various economic opportunities. Some investments were made in Nigeria by some of these investors who found the situation favourable and conducive for commerce. Some countries like US, Britain, G8 generally, that is, group of eight most industrialised nations of the world to which Nigeria was highly indebted, reviewed Nigeria's debt and forgave a significant part of Nigeria's debt. Debt forgiveness by the G8 was seen as one of the greatest achievements of Chief Olusegun Obasanjo.

Economically, the economic policies of Obasanjo's regime were very hostile. He tried to privatise most government parastatals by selling them to the public. Only the rich in the society were able to buy from these parastatals. He approved salary increase for civil servants. In fact, it was generally believed that in the history of Nigeria, the salary package introduced by Obasanjo was the first of its kind that could be really called a living wage. Ironically, this generated a lot of hullabaloo in the various states of the federation as the state governors unanimously refused to implement it. It was a serious battle between the Nigerian Labour Congress and the governors during the time. At the end of the day most states cut down the salary and made their own salary tables for their workers. With the development, people who did the same work in the country earn different salaries even though they go to the same market.

The memory of the wages introduced by Obasanjo was short-lived as he kept on increasing fuel prices. He removed subsidies on petroleum products and made Nigerians to pay more for them. This led to significant increase in the cost of transportation, food, house rent and so on and so forth. The worst part was the price of kerosene which increased tremendously. Kerosene is a household use for the poor masses in Nigeria. During Obasanjo's regime people groaned as they found it difficult to afford the cost of kerosene. Consequently, a lot of people resorted to the use of firewood which they abandoned for years. In years 2004 and 2005 alone Obasanjo increased fuel prices for more than six times. The cost of living generally became very high and people became poorer. The deregulation of oil sector which was one of the major economic policies of Obasanjo brought an unprecedented hardship to the poor masses.

The economic situation of the people was so bad that people started to compare Obasanjo's legitimate regime with the illegitimate regime of General Sanni Abacha. People did this out of pains inflicted on them by Obasanjo's economic policies. It is true that the poor masses suffered in the regime of Obasanjo but, it must be stressed that the policies to some extent led to economic recovery. The external and internal reserve increased. The policy generated money for use. Important projects like road maintenance, construction of roads, education, health to mention a few, received partial attention for the first time after abandonment for many years. Before the death of Abacha or during Abacha's regime, Nigerian roads were a death trap. Obasanjo made sure that most old roads were repaired and new ones awarded for construction. One important thing about Obasanjo's regime that is worth mentioning was the fight against corruption. As soon as Obasanjo assumed power for the second time after his first four years, he made a proclamation that he would step on the toes of many people. And that his regime would have zero tolerance for corruption. Some of those who engaged in corruption practices were brought to book.

Foreign currencies amounting to billions of naira were recovered from Swiss bank and others from the amount stolen from Nigerian treasury by late General Sanni Abacha. This was highly commendable but people were not satisfied or see this as much credit to Obasanjo because the belief was that there were other living ex-Nigerian leaders who stole more money from the treasury than Abacha and they were not touched. People felt that Abacha too would have gone with his loot if not for the fact that he died in office and also that he brutalised Obasanjo while in office

To actualise his dream for a corrupt free Nigeria, he set up two agencies namely the Independent Corrupt Practices (ICPC) and the Economic and Financial Crimes Commission (EFCC). These agencies succeeded in bringing some highly corrupt Nigerian to book. Some of those investigated by the Commission included the former Inspector General of Police, Mr. Tafa

Balogun who was jailed for six months, Professor Fabian Osuji who was relieved of his appointment as the Minister of Education, Alamieseigha who was relieved of his position as Governor of Bayelsa State and jailed, and many other eminent Nigerians. Though, the corruption fighting agencies were alleged by some Nigerians as agents of Obasanjo to fight his enemies, they accused the agents of selective justice. Whether true or false what is important here was the fact that some eminent people were jailed for corruption for the first time.

Politically, Obasanjo could not be called a democrat because the various events that happened during his regime did not portray him as one, due to the role he played. People accused him of playing politics of victimization and flagrant disregard to the rule of law. This accusation was borne out of the fact that he only obeyed those judgements that favoured him, those that did not favour him he refused to obey. An example was the Supreme Court judgement that ordered him to release local government fund for Lagos State. He did not comply with the order. Another court judgement disobeyed by him was the one that requested him to reabsorb back, the university lecturers sacked by the University of Ilorin. More than two years that this judgement had been pronounced, the affected lecturers were not re-absorbed.

People accused him of supporting illegalities by supporting god fatherism in politics. In Anambra State, he supported Chief Uba the political god father of Dr. Chris Ngige who was then the governor of Anambra state against the governor. This led to many ugly situations occuring in Anambra State. First and foremost, the Governor, Chris Ngige was arrested by the Police team led by the Assistant Inspector General of Police Aina and taken out of the government house to an unknown place for more than 24 hours. This arrest was sponsored by Chief Uba the political godfather of Chris Ngige. The misunderstanding that ensued between Uba and Ngige was as a result of failure by Ngige to pay Uba One billion naira from the state government treasury as demanded by Uba.

The arrest of Dr. Ngige was a serious violation of the Nigeria constitution which immunises the governors against arrest. Under the constitution of the Federal Republic of Nigeria (1999) the elected governor cannot be arrested while in power, but this was violated. People expected president Obasanjo who took oath of office to defend the constitution to act rationally but he could not because of his relationship with Uba. The event was unprecedented in the history of Nigeria. It portrayed Nigerians as people who were not politically mature. When this event could not lead to the removal of Chris Ngige from office, Chief Uba hired political thugs who invaded the government house, ministries and parastatals damaging government properties amounting to billions of naira while the police folded their arms watching. The police acted only when Chief Olusegun Obasanjo was interested, anything that did not interest him, no matter how worst, the police would not act. That is to say that the police became partisan during Obasanjo's regime.

The belief of most Nigerians was that Obasanjo was the one that removed governor Ngige. This belief could be said to be true to a large extent because it was indeed unbelievable for a single man to overthrow or hold an elected public office holder like a governor to ransom as did in Anambra and Oyo states. This exercise was a show of shame and a demonstration of political immaturity. It was a breach of the constitution. Every rational thinking Nigerian would not like to remember this ugly incident. It was worse than a military coup. Those who perpetrated this dastardly act were allowed to go scot free because they seem to have the backing of the president.

It was done first in Anambra state, when it succeeded it was also done in Oyo state. Governor Ladoja was removed by his political god father Chief Adedibu. Misunderstanding came up between them when Ladoja was not ready to be a mere figure head and allow Adedibu to be the major player of the game. Also, for disallowing to allow Adedibu to take money from the state treasury as he likes. In this case, Ladoja was not even taken to court before he was removed. The house of assembly, political thugs and the police were used to remove him. Some members of the house of assembly who did not form a quorum were used to remove him, as they already secured the support of the police.

Looking at the way Obasanjo handled political, ethnic and

religious crises, one might be forced to accuse him of partiality. There were instances when the northerners especially those in Kano and Kaduna engaged the other ethnic groups like Igbo and Yoruba in a duel, killing them en masse in the name of religion, event that happened outside the continent of Africa which supposed not to concern Nigerians. For example in 1999 when the Allied forces declared war against Afghanistan because of Osama bin Laden, al-Qaeda leader. U.S and her allies wanted the president of Afghanistan to hand over Osama bin Laden for trial over various terrorist activities perpetrated by him. It was gathered that Bin Laden was based in Afghanistan and that he was being supported by Afghanistan government. When Afghanistan government refused to honour the request and sequent upon the attack of the World Trade Centre in America in September 11, 2001, in which many people both Americans and foreigners lost their lives, Afghanistan was attacked. The aim of this attack was to debase Bin Laden and destabilize the Taliban. That is, the government of Afghanistan her supporter.

As the attack began, riot took place in Kano. Many Igbo and Yoruba people were killed. In fact, thousands of people were killed, and their properties destroyed to the extent that Obasanjo who rushed down from his foreign tour had to shed tears openly. At the end, nothing was done to these murderers. Another crisis was the one which a Spanish based magazine portrayed Prophet Muhammed in a bad way. Everybody condemned the action of this magazine in Nigeria has done in other parts of the world but because it is customary for the people of the north to waste human lives in the name of religion, they declared war against Igbo and Yoruba people. They killed them in thousands in Kano and Kaduna. People would expect Obasanjo's government to take a decisive action that would deter this people from wasting innocent lives but nothing serious was done.

When the Igbo people in the south saw the corpses of their relatives in the north being brought home, they decided to retaliate by starting to kill the northerners in their towns. No sooner they started this than Obasanjo drafted soldiers there to quench the crisis. Those arrested in the crisis were ordered to be taken to court for the first time. But since the north had been doing it, nothing happened. The bone of contention here is that it was like Obasanjo had great fear for the northerners. He always had a kind of soft spot for them and reluctant to take the right step when the northerners were involved.

In terms of regard for fundamental human rights, Obasanjo's record was the best in the history of leadership in Nigeria. His administration was very tolerant. People were free to say what they felt, like and perceive about any national issue. Some even went to the extent of insulting the personality of Obasanjo over the screen calling him all sorts of names and they went free unchallenged. Though, there was a time, two journalists, Aruleba from AIT and Awopetu from Guardian newspaper were arrested and charged to court over the issue of presidential plane newly acquired by the presidency. The plane that was said to be new developed fault on motion not quite two months after it was delivered to Nigeria. The journalists wrote and ran commentary over the television, doubting the authenticity of the plane being new. This marked the first time anybody would be arrested for expressing his opinion. However, one important thing about this was the fact that, they were immediately charged to court and they were granted bail.

One major achievement of Chief Obasanjo was in the area of mobile phone. His deregulation policy broke the monopoly of Nigerian Telecommunication Ltd, and this gave birth to the emergence of various communication companies. Many Nigerians were able to have access to easy communication. Today, you find handsets everywhere in the society. The belief that GSM was for the rich was discarded as people, both rich and poor now have their own personal handsets.

In the area of electricity, no significant success was recorded. Though, electricity was already a thing of the past in most parts of Nigeria as at the time Obasanjo came in. Having identified electricity as a major problem facing industrialisation and industrial activities, he sank billions of naira into National Electricity Power Authority (NEPA) with the aim of reviving it. Upon all, nothing was achieved as NEPA continued total black out and epileptic services. This badly affected industrialisation. Many investors who would have invested in the country could not do so because of lack of regular power supply. Some few industries that were already in place could not operate at full capacity, some even folded up because of the high cost of generating power. However, towards the tail end of his tenure, he ordered for the building of eleven giant power stations and committed billions of naira to it. But most of the contractors only collected the money and failed to do the work.

The international relations of Obasanjo earned him great and first class international reputation. During his tenure, two American presidents visited Nigeria; they were President Bill Clinton and his successor President George W. Bush. He was instrumental to the formation of African Union and was elected the first president. African Union (AU) was used to solve many political problems within and outside African continent. The coup in Principe and Tobago which ousted the incumbent president was reversed as a result of his intervention. Also crises in Liberia, Togo, Congo, Sudan to mention a few were all brought under control as a result of the intervention of Chief Olusegun Obasanjo in his capacity as the African Union President.

Obasanjo hosted presidents of the Common Wealth of Nations during his tenure; he also contributed to the development of sports. He built a gigantic stadium in Abuja. This stadium cost about sixty billion naira and it is one of the largest in Africa. He hosted Common Wealth Games at Abuja during his tenure.

His contribution to agriculture was unprecedented in the

history of Nigeria. Before the advent of Obasanjo as civilian president, agriculture in Nigeria was seen as a profession of the poor. Nobody wanted to go into farming because people felt that it requires hard labour and brought little in terms of returns. He made loan available to the farmers to enable them expand their farmlands. About fifty billion naira (N50, 000,000,000) was set aside as loan for farmers. He ensured that farm produce prices appreciated in the market. Food stuff like gari which was hitherto regarded as a poor man's food because of its cheapness in the market became a rich man's food as the price appreciated. This development was brought about by the discovery of foreign market for cassava. This became one of the major export commodities of Nigeria.

To ensure that farmers get good remunerations for their produce, he banned the importation of those foodstuffs that could be produced locally. This served as an encouragement to the farmers.

He made a significant contribution to education. He increased allocation to the higher institutions by increasing the budget for education. He equipped the teaching hospitals to meet the modern day standard. Before he ascended the throne, the nation's universities were almost becoming glorious secondary schools due to several years of neglect. He released funds for the rehabilitation of dilapidated infrastructures. Though, this was not without the struggle of the various unions within the universities and other higher institutions. Teachers across all levels of Nigerian education were able to earn a fair salary for the first time in the history of the nation during his time.

Another contribution to education was the introduction of Universal Basic Education (UBE), unlike the former system which was based on six years of primary education, three years of junior secondary, three years of senior secondary and four years of university education (6-3-3-4). He based his UBE on a 9-3-4 system. That is, primary education was merged with junior secondary, and was made compulsory for every child. By implication, every child that was born in the nation must finish the first nine years of education before he could talk of not reading again. He ensured the training of teachers for the programme and the retraining of the existing teachers. National Certificate of Education (NCE) holders were recruited en masse into the National Teacher Corps and posted throughout the nation's schools to teach.

The Teacher Registration Council which was to prepare the Nigerian teachers for registration and professionalization was activated. Teachers were registered and issued certificate for the first time. Even though, this Council was not able to bring improvement to the condition of service of the Nigerian teachers, it helped to improve the prestige of Nigerian teachers.

He launched an endowment fund for presidential library which he intended to build in his name at Abeokuta, Ogun State capital. More than seven billion naira was realised at this launching. This idea of the president was criticized by many

Nigerians. Many equated such launching while the president was still in office to corruption. His critics believed that such launching should have come up after his exit from office. They stressed further that most of the people that donated towards the project did so with the intention of compensating the president for one contract or the other or looking for one favour or the other from him. Others felt that the proceeds from such launching should have been diverted towards equipping the libraries of the Nigerian universities which presently were stocked with obsolete text books.

Most Nigerians did not believe that Obasanjo was actually fighting corruption even though some eminent and highly placed government officials were used as scape goats. When Obasanjo left office as a president in 2007, his administration was investigated and high magnitude of corruption was discovered especially in the power sector where billions of dollars were spent on contracts which were either not executed or poorly executed. The amount spent by Obasanjo on electricity was so alarming that his successor Alhaji Musa Yar Adua found it difficult to allocate money to the power sector in the 2008 budget. He claimed that the large amount spent by Obasanjo previously on the power sector did not bear any fruit as there was black out everywhere.

Other area where corruption was discovered in his regime was in the transportation and ports authority. Some of the ministers like Aborisade, Fani-Kayode, Okonjo Iweala to mention a few, were either arrested or invited by investigating committee or Economic and Financial Crime Commission (EFCC) for questioning. It is also very important to stress that Obasanjo's daughter namely Mrs. Iyabo Obasanjo-Bello who was a senator in the next regime after Obasanjo's exit was arrested by EFCC for corruption and charged to court.

In the light of the above, one may rightly say that the anti-corruption crusade of Obasanjo was a ruse due to a number of reasons:

1. The wealth accumulated by Obasanjo was more than his legitimate earning, that is, Obasanjo anti-corruption crusade was utopia and hypocritical because his hands were not clean;

2. His regime featured corrupt Nigerians whose hands were soiled in one corruption or the other;

3. Nigerians will not forget in a hurry the billions of dollars wasted on the power sector without any result;

4. Right from the local government to the federal government a lot of public officers looted the treasury and went scot free;

5. Billions of naira were wasted on the aviation sector construction of roads, and other sectors without anything to show for it.

6. Only the politicians could be said to have enjoyed his regime because of the fabulous salaries and ill gotten wealth while other Nigerians were groaning in poverty, penury and economic hardship.

In conclusion, Obasanjo second tenure was a colossal waste

like that of most of his predecessors. Nigerians were frustrated because they had great hope in somebody like Obasanjo whom God brought from death to life, that he would run a good and Godly government that will ensure equitable distribution of resources and ensure. His performance however fell short of people's expectation as he became more materialistic and worldly than even people who did not go through the difficulty he went through before becoming the civilian president.

CHAPTER SIX: NIGERIAN GOVERNMENT AND THE ISSUE OF CORRUPTION

Introduction

Nigeria is a federation simply because it is practising federalism with federal constitution. Nigeria could also be said to be a democratic state in that it is practising a democratic system of government. It is not an exaggeration that democracy has led to economic progress and prosperity in countries like United States of America, United Kingdom, and some other advanced countries of the world. Perhaps that was the reason for Nigerian's adoption of democracy as a system of government. Ironically, Nigerian democracy seems to have brought poverty and penury to Nigerians.

The question that comes to the mind of every rational thinking person is that, why is democracy not yielding the type of fruits it bears in most advanced countries of the world? Is democracy as a system of government discriminating against colours and races? Or is there any secret of democracy that is not known to Nigerians? The answers to these questions are not farfetched. To adopt a system that is working in another country is not as important as to be able to make the sacrifice that makes it work where it was transferred or imported. The difference between Nigerian democracy and American democracy has to do with Nigerians who are practising the system. Democracy as a system of government does not discriminate between colours or races, but for democracy to work and bring about economic progress and development; those that practise it must imbibe the principle of accountability and probity. Also the principle of subjection of personal interest under the national interest must be upheld. The idiosyncrasy and mentality of an average American or Briton is completely different from that of Nigerians. Every American is ambitious to contribute his or her own quota to the development and economic progress of their nation, and make their nation greater than any country in the world.

The emphasis of Americans is on national development and the strategies of achieving it. While in Nigeria, emphasis seems to be on "I" instead of "we". The spirit of "I" is an anti social, anti-progress, crude and uncivilised spirit. Anywhere in the world, the spirit has not brought or yielded any fruit other than poverty, penury and economic backwardness, with only few corrupt individuals having more than enough, while others languish in the bondage of poverty.

Democracy does not discriminate against colours or races and there is no secret that makes democracy yield good fruit other than sacrifice, accountability, selfless service, subjection of self interest under that of the national interest and genuine love for one's nation. Where these are lacking, reverse seems to be the case. That is exactly what is affecting Nigerians and unless Nigerians (both the leaders and followers) change their mentality and idiosyncrasy, the future of the country and its people seems to be in jeopardy.

Democracy is not a government of corrupt practices, making money into individual pockets or diverting the nation resources into personal uses as being done by majority of Nigerians. The central forces of democracy should be the development of the society. When the society is developed, individual would develop. But the situation with Nigeria is that of few individuals who are opportune to lead the others developing above the nation they rule and the people they lead.

What is Corruption?

Roger (1988) defined corruption as the unauthorized use of public office for private gain. The most common form of corruption is bribery and extortion and the misuse of inside information.

William (1994) sees corruption as immorality, decadence, debauchery, vice, depravity, iniquity, turpitude. It also means dishonesty, fraud and distortion. The encyclopaedia Americana (1995) opined that corruption is a general term for the misuse of public position of trust for private gain.

There are isolated pocket of rectitude, just as there are instances of object venality. Most communities come to tolerate the systematic corruption of their officials through one of three patterns:

1. Non-enforcement of policies for officials high in an organisation

2. Community indifference; and

3. Encouragement by leading citizens

The specific definition and application vary with time, place and culture. Many actions popularly described as corruption may not be so defined in law, although they may constitute a departure from strict ethical standards. The definition of corruption in areas other than politics is also uncertain because of the quasi-public nature of large enterprises in modern capitalist countries, financial manipulations and decisions injurious to the economies of socialist societies. Electoral corruption includes purchase of votes with money, promises of office or special favours, coercion, intimidation and interference with freedom of election. Corruption in office include sale of legislative votes, administrative or judicial decision or governmental appointment, disguise payment in the form of gifts, legal fees, employment favours to relatives, social influence, or any relationship that sacrifices the public interest and welfare, with or without the implied of money, is usually considered corrupt

Political corruption is as old as the history of cultures, system of government or ideologies. Corruption in ancient Greece and Rome increased with their expansion from homogeneous city-states to commercial power and imperial dominion. As it has been stressed, political corruption is not peculiar to any nation or culture, even the developed countries of the world had their own history of corruption period. For instance, in medieval England, the public duty of serving in parliament was so unpopular that men often paid to avoid it. However, with the advent of the tutors, the influence of the parliament increased.

After the restoration of the Stuart Kings in 1660, the king and his opponents competed, not by fighting but by corrupting the parliament in order to further their respective aims. Electoral corruption continued late into the 19th century. Suffrage had been highly and irrationally restricted. Many English and most Irish parliamentary seats were controlled either by influential land owners or boroughs (incorporated urban centres) that were often close corporations dominated by one political party.

To solve the problem of political corruption in England, an effective reform was put in place. A combination of middle class demands aristocratic concern and the needs of political modernization brought reform from above, many reform acts were initiated, and these include the reform act of 1832 and Disraeli's reform law in 1867. Gladstone's in 1884 provided virtually manhood suffrage, which combined with the secret ballot of 1872 to make elections difficult to control. Reporting of electoral spending had been established in 1854, and 14 years later its regulatory was transferred from parliament to the courts.

The corruption and illegal practices act of 1883 carefully prescribed the conduct of election, limited spending, focused responsibility, and set a heavy penalty for violations. To this end, English local government was democratised and protected against corruption by laws such as the reform act and the municipal corporation act of the 1833s, and the corrupt and illegal practices act of 1883 and the parish council's act of 1895. There were also attempts to improve the courts, legal profession, police and penal system. Lord Macaulay's merit system for the India Civil Service in 1833 was copied in 1853 for England. Corruption by military supplies had been attacked by William Pit in 1782, and purchase of rank in the Navy and army was reformed in the next century.

Factors that shaped England's exemplary political system included evangelical Christianity, utilitarian rationalism, middle-class pressure, and the Victorian spirit of morality and public service. Other significant factors were the growth of mass literacy, pressure from reformers and the popular press, the growth of a pragmatic political party system, and strong and often disinterested leadership in parliament.

In Nigeria, corruption is found in all spheres of human endeavour. There is political corruption, economic corruption, religious corruption, financial corruption, administrative corruption, social corruption to mention a few.

Transparency International (an international body), some years ago rated Nigeria as the most corrupt nation in the world. This was during the earlier part of Obasanjo's regime, with the little effort made by Obasanjo's regime to fight corruption, the body later ranked Nigeria as second and later 15th most corrupt nation of the world. The rating by this international body was based on financial perception but corruption goes beyond this. The 2009 rating released in November shows that Nigerian politicians were the highest paid public office holders in the world, while Nigerian workers was adjudged the lowest paid in the world.

Corruption covers all wrong doings that are injurious to the society or capable of bringing the society backward. Corruption in Nigeria would be examined under the categories mentioned above.

Political Corruption: This has to do with politics in Nigeria. For more than two decades, election in Nigeria had been characterised with mass rigging, people could no longer choose a leader they trust but a leader imposed on them by the cabal (ruling class). In essence, election is just a waste because before the day of the election, some people are already aware of who is going to occupy the position.

A lot of money was used for election; politicians distribute money openly to buy the conscience of the people. Apart from the votes there were underground agents that work for them to rig the election. Because the elections are not free and fair, the interest of the masses could not prevail. Instead, the cabal always have their way, in most cases they have the money and the power that be. A situation where the government in power has candidates for various positions makes it difficult in Nigeria for ordinary citizens to win election against the government candidates. The reason for this is simple, the government controls the security apparatus of the state, and it is easy to use this apparatus to rig any election. Another instance is where a person in government is contesting election with an ordinary citizen. Experience has shown that such individual always win the election even where the people voted for the ordinary citizen. In most cases, the government in power make use of state security agent to harass the opponents. This is purely a corrupt behaviour.

Ideally, if people are going to be given a level play ground, that is, equal opportunity, everyone in government who is interested in contesting an election must resign some months to the election. As this is not done in Nigeria, you find out that some credible citizens refused to come out to contest election against the incumbent. Another major political corruption is the idea of using hired assassins to terminate lives of the opponents. This is so rampant in Nigeria. A lot of eminent citizens were killed for political reason. People campaign against military coup, but is there much difference between the military coup and the civilian coup? Both result sometimes to lost of lives. Though, some military coup does not lead to lost of lives. This idea of terminating lives of the opponent is another dangerous dimension in Nigerian politics. This happens because the only way to become rich overnight in Nigeria is through politics. As a politician, you earn fabulous salary; engage in corruption by embezzling public fund. You rarely find a leader in Nigeria who actually possesses genuine interest to serve his people. What is common are leaders who came to power to amass wealth for themselves and members of their immediate families and by the time they are living office, they have become stinking rich that even tenth generation of their offsprings cannot finish what they have stolen.

Politics has been turned to a do or die affair in Nigeria because of the wealth involved, and people are desperate to shed blood of their opponents just to get the leadership position. Those that do not kill, maim and terrorise their opponents with political thugs. Thugs are very cheap to hire in Nigeria because of the high level of poverty ravaging the country. The area boys, garage workers and touts are ready to die with ordinary two hundred naira. Only those who have made up their minds to face the consequences, come out to contest election in Nigeria. That is the more reason why only few credible Nigerians are in politics. No decent Nigerian would like to come out to face the ordeals and danger which Nigeria politics portrays.

Another bad thing about Nigerian politics is the idea of people in government who are also interested in re-contesting an election appointing the electoral officers. Ideally, one would expect the judicial commission to be the one to appoint the National Electoral Chairman and Commissioners, and the money needed for the election should be handed over to the electoral commission without passing through the president. If things are done this way the electoral commission which suppose to be independent, unbiased, unsentimental, incorruptible and be guided by high moral principle, would be able to do their work without taking instruction from the president.

The President or the executive appoints the electoral officers and thus, they owe their loyalty to him, since the allocation for the commission comes directly from the executive and the Executive has the power to fire the electoral officers. The issue is that of he who pays the piper that dictates the tune. In fact, this is one of the reasons why it is easier for election to be rigged in Nigeria. Also connected to this, is the appointment of judges which is done by the executive instead of the judicial commission. In a country where this system is in operation, administration of justice would be affected. Citizens would not be able to enjoy equality before the law and the judgement pronounced in the courts of law would be influenced by power that be.

The electoral tribunals set up by the executive to look into complaints rarely dispense justice without fear or favour. To be frank and sincere, it is not easy for any tribunal to pronounce judgement against the power that set it up. If administration of justice is to be based on truth or devoid of manipulation by the executive, the appointment of judges and electoral commission officers should be purely a business of the judicial commission, and funds should also be through the judicial commission. It is only through this means, that their independence can be guaranteed.

Economic Corruption: This has to do with wrong doings or misbehaviours in the area of economy. It is the illegalities against the economy. These wrong doings or misbehaviours could be itemized as follows:

1.   Defrauding an individual of government;
2.   Giving and collection of bribes;
3.   Inflation of contract fees;
4.   Collection of gratification;
5.   Evasion of taxes
6.   Robbery
7.   Advanced fee fraud known as 419
8.   Incorrect measurement (when selling goods)
9.   Stealing
10.   Refusing to pay debt
11.   Presenting fake product as original to customers
12.   Manufacturing fake products
13.   Importing contraband goods
14.   Smuggling
15.   Pirating
16.   Taking much from someone and paying him less e.g. poor salary;
17.   Collecting money for services not rendered; and so on and so forth

All these and more others not mentioned are so rampant in Nigeria today due to poor administration by the nation's leaders. It is not an exaggeration to say that Nigeria is blessed with adequate natural resources that could make every citizen of the nation to live a comfortable and decent life, but due to the mismanagement, selfishness, self-centredness, egoism, self-aggrandizement, unpatriotic and faulty idiosyncrasy of the nation's so called leaders; citizens find themselves lacking in the midst of plenty and thirsty inside the water.

The military ruled the nation and failed, the civilian ruled the nation still is the same story of failure. The nation's wealth is being enjoyed by a few Nigerians who constituted themselves to a cabal (ruling house). These cabal leaves in Nigeria, they believe in themselves and members of their immediate families. Each of them creates and run individual government outside the nation's government. For example, they have a chain of expensive latest cars and jeeps, they make boreholes for themselves, they procure the best generators to supply electricity, they build mansions and castles, they go abroad for treatment when they are sick and their children attend the best school/universities abroad.

When you talk of lack of electricity, poor medical services, falling standard of education, unemployment to mention a few, they show no concern. People see them and know them. The source of their wealth is well known to the people. The worst part is that people accord those people with questionable wealth great respect as a result of loss of societal values. They are honoured with chieftaincy titles and honorary Doctorate Degrees in the nation's universities, they chairman important occasions/ceremonies, even in the churches they are considered the most religious people because of the donations to the church, and men of God pray for them specially. The effect of this action is that unrighteousness and criminalities are legitimised. Thus people struggle to make money by all means since those who made it through crooked means are now the celebrated heroes and heroines in the society.

Committing crimes and criminal behaviours become order of the day. When the leaders want to talk, they say the teacher should teach morals to the pupils or religious subjects should be made compulsory in schools. All these ideas of the leaders are fallacy with the level of corruption in Nigeria today; the pupil/students would only look at the teacher as hypocrite or somebody preaching impossible doctrine. We have instances when the higher institution students would tell the lecturer of Citizenship Education that what he has said is not practicable in Nigeria.

Moral Corruption: This has to do with anti-moral activities or actions that are against the ideals of the society. Every society has its culture, tradition and custom. There are things which the society cherishes and those that the society detests. It is no more a news that there is cultural disintegration in Nigeria. The values of the society in those days are no longer in vogue. People indulge in activities that the society consider highly anti-social, anti-culture and anti-tradition today. The cause of these is not unconnected with the economic hardship.

A hungry man is an angry man, when poverty has gone to chronic; people are ready to do anything to survive. There is a common saying that it is better to kick the bucket, that is, to die, than to steal, but I want to say categorically that it is not easy for one to agree to die when there is alternative that can make one to survive. A lot of people would prefer to steal and live where it is possible than to die especially in the modern society where pen robbers are the lords in the society and the few honest ones are nowhere to be found.

It must be stressed that not all anti-moral behaviour of people are caused by economic hardship. Some can be traced to the influence of foreign culture. People see western culture as a civilised one and are bent on copying this religiously, without knowing that there are a lot of differences between the western and African culture. For example, it is part of African culture for women or ladies to be well dressed and ensure proper coverage of the body with cloth. This is contrary to the western culture where ladies wearing brassier and pant alone in public is seen as entertainment.

In the past, when a lady dresses shabbily, it is a disgrace to her family as the whole society would criticise this and caution her against such indecent dressing. The following are some elements or items of moral decadence in the society today. These are:

1.   Indecent dressing;
2.   Lack of respect for elders;
3.   Lying;
4.   Bearing false witness;
5.   Adultery;

6.   Disobeying ones parents;

7.   Begging for money/food when one is not a disable;

8.   Laziness;

9.   Insulting someone that is older than you;

10.   Stealing;

11.   A man having fun with man (gay);

12.   Drunkenness;

13.   Lousiness;

14.   Tale bearing;

15.   A man having fun with his relations;

16.   Prostitution;

17.   Pride

18.   Thuggery/fighting

19.   A woman having fun with woman (Lesbian)

20.   Hooliganism; and so on and so forth

If one calls the Nigerian society an immoral society today, he is not insulting us because those behaviours that negate our values and unacceptable to our culture are upheld and perpetrated. In the past, before one would kill another, he would think twice about the consequences, but today, we have professional killers who make killing an occupation. Married women are found offering their bodies for sex by collecting money or favour. Most of the girls are now professional prostitutes.

Professional beggars are ubiquitous, able-bodied men and women go about asking for money instead of engaging in an occupation, some dispossess people of their belongings.

Children no longer respect their parents not to talk of someone older than them. The whole society is in a mess. We are like people without culture. A girl would dress and you see directly the hair in her pubic region. The glory that God gave her that only her husband supposed to see is advertised in public. A man who is not fit to cater for one wife marries three or more wives and starts to manufacture children which he lacks ability to train. These children grow up and serve as thugs to politicians. All these show the extent of moral laxity and decadence in the Nigerian society.

The idea expressed in certain quarters that teachers should teach the pupils/students to be morally upright may not solve the problem as long as those who made it through crook means parade themselves and display their wealth. No amount of explanation given by the teacher would convince the pupils/students except there is correction from the top. Corruption started from the top, that is, high places and flowed down to the low places. If it must be abolished the changes must come from the top. In most cases, leadership determines the followership. When the leadership is corrupt the followership would emulate and replicate the corrupt way of life.

In conclusion, an anti-corruption crusade led by a corrupt man can never succeed except the first surrender everything he has acquired illegally. Otherwise, people would just see him as someone who has stolen enough and is now telling those who have not been opportune to steal something that stealing is not good.

The State of Corruption among the Nigerian Public

Corruption that started from the top many years ago has now eaten deep to the bone and marrow of the followers, the general public. No wonder Transparency International had rated Nigeria in the past as the most corrupt, second most corrupt and later 15th most corrupt nation in the world. Corruption is now the order of the day right from children to adults. The simple reason for this is that, it is conspicuous to all and sundry that most of our wealthy men and women in the society are those who made their money through illegal means. The worst part is that these people go about displaying their ill gotten wealth without any form of opposition or condemnation. Thus, people see corruption as a quick way of amassing wealth.

The situation is really alarming, as you rarely find a truthful person when it comes to money, everyone at his or her level design a mechanism to cheat others. The trader sells an inferior product to his customer and calls it original one. Those selling electrical materials and electronics put an inferior engine in the cover of original one and sell it as original. Market women tamper with their measuring instruments, so as to make the unsuspecting customer get less of their actual purchased product. Those dealing in textile materials cheat their customers by removing some centimetre from the measurement. Motor mechanics tells you that a part of the car has spoilt when actually it is not so. He collects money from you for a new one and later put your own he earlier said was bad for you. Also, when you leave your car with many of them, they remove some parts and replaced with bad ones.

You want to build a house, you ask someone to help you mould blocks, and you give him bags of cement, he would sell some bags and keep the money for himself and over mix the remaining bags with sand to produce the number of bags expected of the total number of real bags of cement. Students cannot read again to pass their examinations. Instead, they pay the invigilators to assist them hire mercenaries to do the examination for them. That is the reason why a lot of certificate holders in Nigeria today cannot defend or behave in consonance with the skills the certificate conveys. Teachers/lecturers breach the rules of examination by giving marks to undeserved students either because they have collected money from them or the female student has released her body to the lecturer.

Everyone is desperate to make it. No more honest person again when it comes to money. Internet fraudsters fill everywhere, dupers are not left out. Civil servants/public servants use their offices to make money into their pockets. Contract fees are inflated; contractors use inferior materials and execute poor quality jobs because certain percentage of the contract fees had been collected by those who awarded the contract and party members. Hence, you see a road constructed or repaired within a year full of port-holes. The revenue collectors like the customs, collect half into the public treasury and half into their pockets that is the reason why most big mansions and expensive cars/jeeps belong to custom officers or politicians.

They claim they are fighting smugglers and they are the one aiding them. The seizures announced over the radio and television are those who cannot meet the condition given to them. Those who are ready to pay are allowed to go scot free. Another worst government organisation is the so called Power Holding Company of Nigeria (PHCN). Workers of this organisation or parastatal have constituted themselves into the enemies of the country because of their corrupt practices. They go from house to house to collect bribe. They prefer people to settle them than to pay the bill, they tamper with transformers so as to collect money from the people. They distribute money on every house as bill which they must pay whether they use electricity or not. They forge meter readings for customers, they bring crazy bills to customers, they collude with unscrupulous people to steal PHCN facilities, they ally with generator sellers to see that their business is booming by making power supply irregular. In fact, I doubt it if any effort by government to solve electricity problem in Nigeria can succeed with this crop of criminals working as PHCN staffs.

The health sector is not left out of corruption, Doctors and Nurses in the government hospitals collect bribe before they attend to those that need medical attention. No matter the pains one is going through, unless you are ready to offer bribe, they would be looking at you, abusing you where they need to assist, they lack mercy. One sometimes think whether these people are actually human beings, they have no sympathy, no human feelings and regard for human lives.

The leaders of the nation sowed the seed of corruption and it has germinated, matured and is bearing fruits today. The entire society has been infected with corruption, and this corruption has stagnated the growth of the socio-economic structure of the nation. Year in year out the situation is getting worse. There is no way a corrupt nation like Nigeria can attain greatness. The effect of corruption is now felt in all aspects of the nation's life. Electricity is totally grounded lot of industries have folded up due to high cost of running generator. A lot of foreign investors find it difficult to invest in Nigeria because electricity is vital to any investment. The worst part is that some investors have moved their investment out of Nigeria to the neighbouring country like Ghana, where there is regular supply of power. Nigerian roads are death traps. We read on the newspapers that billions of naira was spent on repair of roads and generation of power right from the time of Chief Olusegun Obasanjo but this money went to private pockets. This is more so as there is nothing on ground to show for such amount of money.

Nigerian education is in crises, most graduates from Nigerian higher institutions according to private sector are said not to be employable. Foreign universities are no longer admitting

Nigerian graduates direct into their post graduate programmes without a remedial course. There is rarely any session that teachers/lecturers do not go on strike over poor welfare packages/infrastructure in the schools/colleges/universities. As at 2009, no university in Nigeria was among the best 200 universities in the world. The money released for education improvement is embezzled between those who release it and those that they released it to. The relationship between the Nigerian government and that of the teachers is like that of slave and his master. Teachers are not considered as human beings that have the right to enjoy good things of life but labourers who should just be given something to keep his life. Whatever he is given he is expected to shut up his mouth. No wonder, rarely can you find a teacher that has the interest of the pupils at heart like that of old. We cannot blame the teachers for devoting their attention on other activities that would fetch them money, because teachers must train their children like any other Nigerian parents. They need food, Shelter and other necessities of life. Since what they are paid and the opportunities available to them as teachers cannot achieve this for them or make them far from achieving this, they have to look for other means of achieving them.

As observed by Asoga-Allen (2002) any job a man does and cannot feed his family or make ends meet will never take his full attention. Until the issue of good condition of service for Nigerian teachers is addressed and teachers are motivated physically, psychologically, emotionally and financially, all the proclamations of the government towards improving education would be seen as a mere lip service.

As dangerous as the issue of corruption is, it retards the progress of any nation that embraces it. For example, who would believe that China and Nigeria obtained their independence almost at the same time? Can we compare the level of development of China with that of Nigeria today? They are far from each other. It has come to the extent that people see Nigeria as a country without future. This is so because Nigerians, especially the masses are groaning under bondage of poverty which the past and present leaders have put them. As at today, only the politicians and their few allies who benefit directly from them claim that all is well with Nigeria. Nigerians have been subjected to all sorts of economic measures in the past. For example there was a time, the government adopted Austerity Measure (AM), Structural Adjustment Programme (SAP), removal of subsidy on feeding of Nigerian students in tertiary institutions, removal of subsidy on petroleum products, retrenchment of workers to mention a few. All these measures have not brought any economic development.

It must also be stressed that the various periods of oil boom experienced by the nation, only the one witnessed during the time of Yakubu Gowon (the then military head of state) brought meaningful change in the condition of living of Nigerians. It has always been that those in government are worthy of millions/billion while masses lavish in poverty and penury, that is the effect of corruption. At the inception of a new government, promises of a number of programmes always follow. Nigeria has always been one of the first signatories to a number of world declarations in respect of economic and educational development when the nations of the world formulated a new treaty. All these have been found to be mere paper work that would not record any success. Nigeria is one of the few nations in the world where the leaders are only interested in themselves and self-interest, rather than the general interest of those who voted them to power.

It has reached the climax where people acquire political office whether they win elections or not. They do this through election rigging and assassination of opponents. It is certain that a leader that ascended the throne through fraudulent means would not be accountable to the people but those who assisted him in perpetrating the nefarious action. That is exactly what is happening in Nigeria. Those who donated money for an election to be rigged and make wrong candidates to emerge as winners in Nigeria control the economy of the nation. The economic future of millions of Nigerians is committed to their hands. The importation of most essential goods is handled by these few exceptionally and stinking rich men and they sell to Nigerians at any amount they like, and make billions from Nigerians.

The handwriting is clear on the wall that these bourgeoisies have not good plan for Nigeria and the people. They are not only interested in what they can get from the nation. They have nothing to contribute. In fact, to every rational thinker, Nigeria is in trouble considering the natural resources available in the country and number of years the nation has obtained her political independence. The leaders of the nation have eaten and are eating the portion of the masses with their own. The worst affected are the youths in Nigeria. Their future seems very bleak in the hands of these bloody corrupt leaders. For example, while a bag of cement is being sold for between N1, 700 and N2, 200 in Nigeria, it is being sold for N1000 in Togo, a country that has not up to one-tenth the resources of Nigeria. Because the man importing this commodity is a money bag and one of the king makers, all the promises of the president and Commander in chief Alhaji Yar adua to bring the price of the product to N1000 was just a talk of the mouth; not only cement but prices of other essential goods. The questions are how long are Nigerians going to be held hostage by the unscrupulous politicians and their allies? Who is going to liberate Nigerians from the hands of these few percentage of the population that are holding them hostage? The answer belongs to God, but one thing is certain, that is the fact that Nigerians should forget about it that any good thing can come out from these crop of people ruling us. This is because they are already accustomed to corruption and legitimized it as a way of life.

Millions of youths who graduated from poorly equipped

higher institutions are roaming the street; the government is paying leap service to the matter of employment generation. Many youths die daily in an attempt to enter another country illegally, many turned to armed robbery, kidnapping, ritual killing, internet fraud, prostitution to mention a few, and the government is contented with the state of the nation. They see nothing wrong in it since their biological children are comfortable at home and abroad.

Nigerian leaders have to learn from other nations or history. No nation can continue this way for ever. One day the oppressed who hitherto fear death would be ready to die, we have started to see traces of this. The Niger-Delta youths in the southern and eastern parts of the nation have carried arms against the government. This emerged out of many years of marginalization which led to frustration. The evil effects of oppressive government are enormous. For example, apart from militant group emerging, there are other associating evils like kidnapping and armed robbery.

CHAPTER SEVEN: NIGERIAN DEMOCRACY AND GLOBALIZATION

Introduction

Globalization is the process by which the people of the world are unified into a single society in order to function together. Globalization is often used to refer to economic globalization: the integration of national economies into the international economy through trade, foreign direct investment, capital flow, migration and the spread of technology. This process is usually recognised as being driven by a combination of economic, technological, socio-cultural, political and biological factors. The term can also refer to the transnational dissemination of ideas, languages or popular culture.

The term globalization "has been in the social sciences since the 1960s. However, the term did not achieve wide spread use until the latter half of the 1980s. An early description of globalization was penned by the American entrepreneurs - turned Minister Charles Taze Russel who coined the term "corporate giants" in 1897. Since its polarization by economists and journalists in the 1980s and 1990s, the concept of globalization has inspired numerous competing definitions and interpretations.

Saskia Sassen writes that

> "a good part of globalization consist of an enormous variety of micro processes that begin to denationalize what had been

constructed as national - whether policies, capital, political, sub-activities, urban space, temporal frames or any other of the variety of dynamics and domains"

Tom G. Palmer of the Cato Institute defines globalization as the elimination of state enforced restrictions on exchanges across borders and increasingly integrated and complex global system of production and exchange that has emerged as a result.

History of Globalization

The historic origins of globalization are the subject of on-going debate. Though some scholars situate the origin of globalization in the modern era, others regard it as a phenomenon with a long history. Perhaps, the most extreme proponent of a deep historical origin for globalization was Adrew Gunder Frank, an economist associated with dependency theory. Frank argued that a form of globalisation has been in existence since the rise of trade link between Sumer and the Indus valley civilization in the third millennium B.C. Critics of the idea point out that it rest upon an overly broad definition of globalization.

Others have perceived an early form of globalization in the trade links between the Roman Empire, the Persian Empire and the Han dynasty. The increasing articulation of commercial links between these powers inspired the development of the Silk Road, which started in China, reached the boundaries of the Persian Empire and continue towards Rome. The Islamic golden age was also an important early stage of globalization, when muslim traders and explorers established a sustained economy across the old world resulting in a globalisation of crops, trade knowledge and technology. The advent of the Mongol Empire, though destabilizing to the commercial centres of the middle East and China, created a great integration along the silk Road which permitted travellers such as Marco polo to journey successfully (and profitably) from one end of Eurasia to the other. These pre-modern phases of global or hemispheric exchange are sometimes known as archaic globalization.

The sixteenth century witnessed a qualitative difference in the patterns of globalization because it was the first period in which the new world began to engage in substantial cultural, material and biological exchange with Africa and Eurasia. This phase is sometimes known as proto-globalization. It was characterised by the rise of maritime European empires, particularly the Portuguese Empire, the Spanish Empire, and later the British and Dutch Empires. It can be said to have begun shortly before the turn of 16th century, when the two kingdoms of the Iberian Peninsula- the kingdom of Portugal and the Kingdom of Castile, began to send explorative voyages to the Americas and around the Horns of Africa. This new sea route permitted sustained contact and trade between the entire world's inhabited regions for the first time.

Global integration continued through the European trade in the 16th and 17th centuries, when the Portuguese and Spanish Empires colonized the Americas followed eventually by France and England. Globalization has had a tremendous impact on cultures particularly indigenous cultures, around the world. In the fifteen century, Portugal's company of Guinea was one of the first chartered commercial companies established by Europeans in other continents during the age of discovery, whose task was to deal with the spices and to fix the prices of the goods

In the 17th century, globalization became a business phenomenon when the British, East India Company (Founded in 1600) which is often described as the first multi-national corporation was established, as well as the Dutch East India Company (founded in 1602) and the Portuguese East India Company (founded in 1628). Because of the large investment and financing needs and the high risks involved with international trade, the British India Company became the first company in the world to share risk and enable joint ownership of companies through the issuance of shares of stocks; an important driver for globalization. Globalization was achieved by the British Empire (the largest Empire in history) due to its share size and power. British ideals and culture were imposed on other nations during this period.

The 19th century is sometimes called "The first era of Globalization" it was a period characterised by rapid growth in international trade and investment between the European imperial powers, their colonies and later, the United States. It was in this period that area of sub-Sahara Africa and the Island Pacific were incorporated into the world system. The "First era of Globalization" began to break down at the beginning of the 20th Century with the First World War said John Maynard Keynes:

> "The inhabitant of London would order by telephone, sipping his morning tea, the various products of the whole earth, and reasonably expect their early delivery upon his doorstep. Militarism and imperialism of racial and cultural rivalries were little more than the amusements of his daily newspaper. What an extra-ordinary episode in the economic progress of man was that age which came to an end in August 1914"

The "First era of Globalization" later collapsed during the gold standard crises and Great Depression in the late 1920s and early 1930s. In early 2000s much of the industrialized world entered into a deep recession. Some analysts say the world is going through a period of de-globalization after years of increasing economic integration. Up to 45% of global wealth had been destroyed by the global financial crises in little less than a year and a half.

Modern Globalization

Globalization, since World War II, is largely the result of planning by politicians to breakdown borders hampering trade to increase prosperity and interdependence thereby decreasing the chance of future war. Their work led to the Bretton Woods Conference, an agreement by the world's leading politicians to lay down the framework for international commerce finance, and the founding of several international institutions intended to oversee the process of globalization.

These institutions include the World Bank and the International Monetary Fund (IMF). Globalization has been facilitated by advances in technology which have reduced the costs of trade and trade negotiation rounds, originally under the auspices of the General Agreement on Tariffs and Trade (GATT) which led to a series of agreements to remove restrictions on free trade.

Since World War II, barriers to international trade have been considerably lowered through international agreements - GATT. Particular initiative carried out as a result of GATT and the World Trade Organisation (WTO), for which GATT is the foundation, has included:

☞ Promotion of free trade;
☞ Elimination of tariffs; creation of free trade zones with small or no tariffs;
☞ Reduced transportation costs, especially resulting from development containerization for ocean shipping
☞ Reduction or elimination of capital controls
☞ Reduction, elimination, or harmonization of subsidies for local businesses
☞ Creation of subsidies for global corporations

☞   Harmonization of intellectual laws across the majority of states with more restrictions

☞   Supranational recognition of intellectual property restrictions (e.g. patents granted by China would be recognized in the United States)

Cultural globalization, driven by communication technology and the worldwide marketing of western cultural industries, was understood at first as a process of homogenization, as a global domination of American culture at the expense of traditional diversity. However, a contrasting trend soon became evident in the emergence of movement protesting against globalization and giving new momentum to the defence of local uniqueness, individually, and identity, but largely without success.

The Uruguay Round (1986 to 1994) led to a treaty to create the WTO to mediate trade disputes and set up a uniform platform of trading. Other bilateral and multilateral trade agreements, including sections of Europe's Maastricht Treaty and the North American Free Trade Agreement (NAFTA) have also been signed in pursuit of the goal of reducing tariffs and barriers to world exports rose from 8.5% of gross world product in 1970 to 16.1% of gross world product in 2001.

Measuring Globalization

Looking specifically at economic globalization, demonstrates that it can be measured in different ways. These centre on the four main economic flows that characterised globalization:

☞ Goods and services e.g. exports plus imports as a proportion of national income or per capital of population;

☞ Labour/people e.g. net migration rates, inward or outward migration flows; weighed by population

☞ Technology e.g. international research and development flows; proportion of population (and rate of change thereof) using particular inventions (especially "factor-neutral" Technological advances such as the telephone, motorcar, broadband)

As globalization is not only an economic phenomenon, a multivariate approach to measuring globalization is the recent index calculated by the Swiss think tank KOF. The index measures the three main dimensions of globalization, economic, social and political. In addition to three indices measuring these dimensions an overall index of globalization and sub-indices referring to actual economic flows, economic restrictions, data on personal contact, data on information flows and data on cultural proximity is calculated. Data is available on a yearly basis for some countries, as detailed in Dreher, Gaston and Martens (2008). According to the Index, the world most globalised country is Belgium, followed by Austria, Sweden, the United Kingdom and the Netherlands. The least globalized countries according to KOF - Index are Haiti, Myanmar, the Central Africa Republic and Burundi. According to A. T, Keaney and Foreign policy magazine (2006) Singapore, Ireland, Switzerland, the Netherlands, Canada, and Denmark are the most globalized, while Indonesia, India and

Iran are the least globalized among countries listed.

Effects of Globalization

Globalization has various aspects which affect the world in several different ways such as:

☞ Industrial - emergence of worldwide production markets and broader access to a range of foreign products for consumers and companies particularly movement of materials and goods between and within national boundaries;

☞ There emerged a worldwide financial markets and better access to external financing for borrowers. As this worldwide structures grew more quickly than any transactional regulatory regime, the instability of the global financial infrastructure dramatically increased, as evidenced by the financial crisis of the 2008.

☞ Economic - realization of a global common market based on the freedom of exchange of goods and capital. The interconnectedness of these markets, however meant than an economic collapse in any one given country could not be contained;

☞ Political: some use "globalization" to mean the creation of a world government which regulates the relationships among governments and guarantees the rights arising from social and economic globalization. Politically, the United States has enjoyed a position of power among the world powers; in part because of the strong and wealthy economy with the influence of globalization and with the help of the United States own economy, the People's Republic of China have experienced some tremendous growth within the past decade. If China continues to grow at that rate projected by the trends, then it is very likely that in the next twenty years, there will be a major reallocation of power along the world leaders. China will have enough wealth, industry and technology to rival the United States for the position of leading the world power.

☞ Informational - increase in information flow between geographically remote location. Arguably, this is technological change with the advent of fibre optic communications, satellites and increased availability of telephone and internet.

☞ Language - the most popular language is English

☞ About 35% of the world's e-mail, telexes and cables are in English

☞ Approximately 40% of the world's radio programmes are in English

☞ About 50% of all internet traffic uses English

☞ Competition - Survival in the new global business market calls for improved productivity and increase competition. Due to the market becoming worldwide, companies in various industries have to upgrade their products and use technology skilfully in order to face increased competition

☞ Ecological - the advent of global environmental

challenges that might be solved with international cooperation, such as climate change, cross boundary water and air pollution, over-fishing of the ocean, and the spread of invasive species. Since many factories are built in developing countries with less environmental regulation, globalism and free trade may increase pollution. On the other hand, economic development historically required a "dirty" industrial stage, and it is argued that developing countries should not, via regulation, be prohibited from increasing their standard of living

☞ Cultural - growth of cross-cultural contacts; advent of new categories of consciousness and identities which embodies cultural diffusion, the desire to increase one's standard of living and enjoy foreign product and ideas, adopt new technology and practices and participate in a "World Culture". The cultural transformation that accompanies this includes spreading of multiculturalism and better individual access to cultural diversity e.g. through the export of Hollywood and Bollywood movies. Some consider such "imported" culture a danger, since it may supplant the local culture, causing reduction in diversity or even assimilation. Others consider multi-culturalism to promote peace and understanding between peoples

☞ Greater international travel and tourism WHO estimates that up to 50,000 people are on place at any time

☞ Greater immigration including illegal immigration

☞ Spread of local consumer products (e.g. food) to other countries (often adopted to their culture)

☞ Worldwide fads and pop culture such as pokemon, sudoku, Numa Numa, Origami, Idol series, You Tube, Orkut, Facebook and Myspace. Accessible to those who have internet or Television, Carving out a substantial segment of the earth's population

☞ Worldwide sporting events such as FIFA world cup and the Olympic Games

☞ Incorporation of multinational corporation into new media. As the sponsor of the All-Blacks rugby team, Adidas had created a parallel website with a downloadable interactive rugby game for its fans to play and compete

☞ Social: development of system of non-governmental organisations as main agents of global public policy, including humanitarian aid and developmental efforts.

☞ Technical

☞ Development of a global telecommunications infrastructure and greater trans-border data flow, using such technologies as the internet, communication satellites, submarine fibre optic cable and wireless telephones

☞ Increase in number of standards applied globally; e.g. Copyright laws, patterns and world trade agreement

☞ Legal/Ethical

☞ The creation of international criminal court and

international justice movement

☞ Crime importation and raising awareness of global crime fighting efforts and cooperation

Cultural Effects

The internet breaks down cultural boundaries across the world by enabling easy, near instantaneous communication between people anywhere in a variety of digital forms and media. The internet is associated with the process of cultural globalization because it allows interaction and communication between people with very different life styles and from very different cultures. Photo sharing websites allow interaction even where language would otherwise be a barrier.

Someone in America can be eating Japanese noodles for lunch while someone in Sydney Australia is eating classic Italian meatballs. One classic culture aspect is food. India is known for their curry and exotic spices, Paris is known for its cheeses. America is known for its burgers and fries. McDonalds was once an American favourite with its cherry mascot, Ronald, red and Yellow theme, and greasy fast food. Now it is global enterprise with 31,000 locations worldwide with locations in Kuwait, Egypt and Malta. This restaurant is just one example of food going big on the global scale.

Mediation has been a sacred practice for centuries in Indian culture. It calms the body and helps one connect to their inner being while shying away from their conditioned self. Before globalization, Americans did not mediate or practice yoga.

After globalization, this is a common practice; it is even considered a chick way to keep your body in shape. Some people are even travelling to India to get the full experience themselves. Another common practice brought about by globalization would be Chinese symbols tattoos. These specific tattoos are a huge hit with today's younger generation and are quickly becoming norm. With the melting of cultures using another country's language in one's body art is now considered normal.

Culture is defined as patterns of human activity and the symbols that give these activities significance. Culture is what people eat, how they dress, beliefs they hold, and activities they practice. Globalization has joined different cultures and made it into something different.

Pro-Globalization

Supporters of free trade claim that it increases economic prosperity as well as opportunity, especially among developing nations, enhances civil liberties and lead to a more efficient allocation of resources. Economic theories of comparative advantage suggest that free trade leads to a more efficient allocation of resources, with all countries involved in the trade benefiting. In general, this leads to lower prices, more employment, higher output and a higher standard of living for those in developing countries.

One of the ironies of the recent successes of India and China is the fear that success in these two countries comes at the expense of the United States. These fears are fundamentally wrong and, even worse, dangerous. They are wrong because the world is not a zero-sum struggle but rather is a positive-sum opportunity in which improving technologies and skills can raise living standards around the world (Jeffery, 2005).

Dr. Francisco Stipo, Director of the USA Club of Rome suggests that "the world government should reflect the political and economic balances of the world nations. A world confederation would not supersede the authority of the state governments but rather complement it, as both the states and the world authority would have power within sphere of competence"

Proponent of Laissez-fair capitalism, and some libertarians, says that higher degree of political and economic freedom in the form of democracy and capitalism in the developed world are ends in themselves and also produce higher level of material wealth. They see globalization as the beneficial spread of liberty and capitalism. Supporters of democratic globalization are sometimes called pro-globalists. They believe that the first phase of globalization, which was market-oriented, should be followed by a phase of building global political institutions representing the will of world citizens. The difference from other globalists is that they do not define in advance any ideology to orient this will, but would leave it to the free choice of those citizens via a democratic process.

Some, such as form Canadian Senator Doughlas Roche, simply

view globalization as inevitable and advocate creating institutions such as a directly-elected United Nations Parliamentary Assembly to exercise oversight over unelected international bodies. Supporters of globalization argued that the anti-globalization movement uses anecdote evidence to support their protectionist view, whereas worldwide statistics strongly support globalization

From 1981 to 2001, according to World Bank figures, the number of people living on $1 dollar a day or less declined from 1.5 billion to 1.1 billion in absolute terms. At the same time, the world population increased, so in percentage terms the number of such people in developing nations declined from 40% to 20% of the population. With the greatest improvements occurring in economies rapidly reducing barriers to trade and investment, yet, some critics argued that more detailed variables measuring poverty should be studied instead.

The percentage of people living on less than $2 dollars a day has decreased greatly, increase in areas affected by globalization, whereas, poverty rate in other areas have remained largely stagnant. In East Asia, including China, the percentage has decreased by 50.1% compared to a 2.2% increase in sub-Saharan Africa

Anti-Globalization

The anti-globalization movement is a term used to describe

the political group who opposed to neoliberal version of globalization, while criticising of globalization are some of the reasons used to justify this group stance. Anti-globalization may also involve the processes or actions taken by a state in order to demonstrate his sovereignty and practice democratic decision making. Anti-globalization may occur in order to maintain barrier to the international transfer of people, goods and beliefs, particularly free market deregulation, encouraged by some organizations such as the IMF or WTO. Moreover, as Naomi Klein argues in her book No Logo Anti-globalism can denote either a single socialism movement or an umbrella term that encompasses a number of separate social movements such as Nationalists and Socialists. In either case, participants stand in opposition to the unregulated power of large, multi-national corporations as the corporation exercise power through leveraging trade agreements which in some instances damage the democratic rights of citizens, the rights including the right to form a union, and health and safety legislation, or laws as they may otherwise infringe on cultural practices and traditions of developing countries.

Some people who are labelled "anti-globalists" or Sceptics according to Hirst and Thompson (2002) considered the term to be too vague and inaccurate. Podobnik states that "the vast majority of groups that participate in these protests draw on international network of support and they generally call for forms of globalization that enhance democratic representation, human rights and egalitarianism".

Joseph and Andrew (2005) write:
The anti-globalization movement developed in opposition of the perceived negative aspects of globalization. The term globalization is in many ways a misnomer, since the group represents a wide range of interests and issues and many of the people involved in the anti-globalization movement do not support closer ties between the various peoples and cultures of the world through, for example, aid assistance for refugees, and global environmental issues.

Some members' aligned with this view point prefer instead to describe themselves as the global justice movement, the Anti-corporate-Globalization movement, the movement of movements (a popular term in Italy), the Aker-globalization movement (popular in France), "the counter globalization" movement and others.

Critiques of the current wave of economic globalization typically look at both the damage to the planet, in terms of the perceived unsustainable harm done to the biosphere, as well as the perceived human costs, such as poverty, inequality miscegenation, injustice and the erosion of traditional culture which the critic contend all occur as a result of economic transformation related to globalization. The challenge directly the metrics, such as GDP, used to measure progress promulgated by institutions such as the World Bank, and look to other measures, such as the Happy Planet Index, created by the new economics foundation. They point to a multitude of interconnected fatal consequences, social disintegration, a breakdown of democracy, more rapid and extensive deterioration of the environment, the spread of new diseases, increasing poverty and alienation but very real consequences of globalization.

Critiques argue that:

☞ **Poorer Countries Suffer Disadvantages**: While it is true that globalization encourages free trade among countries, there are also negative consequences because some countries try to save their national markets. The main export of poorer countries is usually agricultural goods. Larger countries often subsidize their farmers (Like the EU) Common Agricultural Policy, which lowers the market price for the poor farmers crops compared to what it would be under free trade.

☞ **Exploitation of Foreign Impoverished Workers**: The deterioration of protection of weaker nations by stronger industrialized powers has resulted in the exploitation of the people in those nations to become cheap labour. Due to the lack of protections, companies from powerful industrialized nations are able to offer workers enough salary to entice them to endure extremely long hours and unsafe working conditions, though economic question if consenting workers in competitive employers market can be described as "exploited". It is true that the workers are free to leave their jobs but in many poorer countries, this would mean starvation for the workers, and possible even his/her family if their previous jobs were unavailable.

☞ **The Shift to Outsourcing:** The low cost of offshore workers have enticed corporation to buy goods and service from foreign countries. The laid off manufacturing sector workers are forced into service sector where wages and benefits are low, but turnover is high. This has contributed to the deterioration of the middle class which is a major factor in the increasing economic inequality in the United States, and many other countries of the world. Families that were once middle class are forced into lower positions by massive layoffs and outsourcing to another country. This also mean that people in the lower class have a much harder time climbing out of poverty because of the absence of the middle class as a stepping stone.

☞ **Weak Labour Unions:** The surplus in cheap labour coupled with an overgrowing number of companies in transition has caused a weakening of labour unions in the United States. Unions lose their effectiveness when their membership begins to decline. As a result, unions hold less power over corporations that are able to easily reduce workers, often for lower wages and have the option not to offer unionized jobs anymore.

☞ **Increased Exploitation of Child Labour:** For example, a country that is experiencing increase in labour command because of globalization and an increase in demand for goods produced by children will experience greater a demand for child labour. This can be hazardous or exploitative e.g. quarrying, salvage, cash cropping, but also includes the trafficking of children, children in bondage or forced labour, prostitution, pornography and other illicit activities.

One of the key points made by critics of recent economic globalization is that income inequality both between and within nations, is increasing as a result of these processes. One article from 2001 found that significantly, 7 out of 8 metrics, income inequality has increased in the twenty years ending 2001. Also incomes in the lower deciles of world income distribution have probably fallen absolutely since the 1980s. Furthermore, the World Bank Figures on obsolete poverty were challenged. The article was sceptical of the World Bank's claim that the number of people living on less than $1 a day has held steady at 1.2 billion from 1987 to 1998 because of biased methodology.

A chart that give the inequality a very visible and comprehensive for the so called champagne glass effect was contained in the 1992 United Nations Development Programme report, which showed the distribution of global income to be very uneven with the richest 20% of the world's population controlling 82.7% of the world's income.

+ Distribution of the World GDP 1989

Quintile of Population	Income
Richest 20%	82.7%

Second 20%	11.7%
Third 20%	2.3%
Fourth 20%	1.4%
Poorest 20%	1.2%

Source: *UNDP 1992 Human Development Report*

Globalization and Nigerian Economy

Nigeria is an active participant in globalization, there is no doubt that globalization has opened up Nigeria like any other nations to international communities. The products and resources available in Nigeria are made known to the international communities. More Nigerian products especially the agricultural products, like garri, cassava, planks, to mention a few were in high demand by some foreign nations. However, the exportation of these lines of products seems to have aggravated the suffering and rate of poverty among Nigerians. This is because, people sell what they produce that are not even enough for home consumption abroad. This brought about scarcity, inflation of prices and hunger on the people of the nation.

Ideally, what is expected to be sold in international trade is the excess or surplus produce, that is, the one meant for local consumption are already secured, but that is not the case with Nigeria, people produce and take to the international market without minding the home consumption. Take for instance, Garri which was regarded some years ago as a poor man's food, as a result of globalization and the high demand for cassava by the outside world, garri had become a rich man's food. It has gone out of reach of the poor.

To be sincere, Nigeria is not ripe for exportation of agricultural produce because the production level was and still very low. This is so because, most Nigerian farmers are peasant farmers, the size of their farmland is so small; it can only support family consumption with little or nothing to sell in the market. Agriculture is yet to be mechanized in Nigeria due to the level of science and technological development, also for the fact that imported technologies are costly to transfer and maintain. In essence, exportation of the few available agricultural produce in Nigeria has brought suffering on Nigerians than pleasure.

The major export of Nigeria which is the crude oil was sold and being sold in large quantity and a lot of money generated or accrued to the government of the nation. However, it is painful to say that most Nigerians only heard it over the media that billions of dollar were sold and realised by the federal government on a yearly basis, it did not translate into good condition of living for the average Nigerians. In fact, the condition of living is getting worse on a yearly basis. The services that are expected of the government to give to citizens are not performed. In most parts of Nigeria, there is nothing to show that the nation has government except the agents of the government who go about demanding taxes from the economically injured citizens and adding more to their injuries.

Essential social services like electricity, good roads, good schools, provision of portable water and so on and so forth become an individual's affair. The poverty rate was and is very alarming. No job opportunities created by the government and the tertiary institutions are turning out graduates on a yearly basis. Workers are poorly paid, there are workers strike here and there pressing for better condition of living.

Globalization has really increased the gap between the haves and the have-nots. It is observed that while the global wealth has increased, it has become concentrated in the hand of few privileged individuals and few countries. According to Awake (2002) the worth of the 200 riches peoples on wealth on earth now exceed the combined income of 40% of the people who live on the planet 2 - 4 billion of people. It continues further that while wages continues to rise in wealthy countries, 80 impoverished countries have actually seen a decline in average income over the past ten years. Nigeria is among these eighty countries.

The distribution of global wealth has never been fair. But economic globalization has widened the gap between the rich and poor nations. However, some developing countries as observed by Salimono (1999) has benefited from their integration into the global economy. For example, India and Asia as a whole have seen improvement. He noted that only 15% of the East Asian population lives on $1 a day compared with 27% ten years earlier. However, the story is different in Africa and particularly in Nigeria where income has actually decrease community allows nearly 3 billion people - almost half of all humanity - to subsist $2 or less per day in a world of unprecedented wealth. Such gross unfairness - in the global neighbourhood clearly show many seeds of unrest and frustration.

In an interdependent world economy, any adverse global shock affects other countries. For example, the oil glut of 1982 and 1988 according to Salimono (1999) is more rapidly propagated. The propagation mechanism at work can be a decline in the import volume and change in the real price of commodities (oil). Nigeria depends heavily on crude oil as the main source of income or foreign exchange earnings. Her revenue is always hit hard by these shocks (Doguwa and Englana, 2002)

Furthermore, highly integrated financial market tends to transmit global, regional, national or local shock much more rapidly than in past decades when financial markets were less integrated. It has been observed by CBN (2002) that portfolio shift affect the exchange and interest rates including other economic activities. As a consequence, the volumes of financial intermediation and currency transactions are enormous nowadays.

The shocks are greatly amplified in more or less synchronized fashion with destabilizing effects on Nigerian economy. This financial volatility was largely unknown in the 1950s, 1960s, early 1970s when multilateral lending aids and foreign direct investment dominated global capital investment (CBN, 2000).

The effect of globalization is the fear of uncertainty and volatility on capital formation and productivity growth with its negative consequence on economic growth. CBN (2000) viewed the instability on the economy as tax on growth and prosperity. It should be noted that this problem of uncertainty is not from within but externally generated. According to Yusuf (2003) Nigeria as a developing country has not evolved a mechanism that can absorb the shocks generated by the effects of globalization. The type of domestic policy response put in place by the government has increased the negative impact of these shocks in Nigeria and the people are worse off. The income of the people of Nigeria is low and they are living below poverty line.

The social effect of globalization is another fear entertained by Dani (1997) when he states that since globalization is associated with instability of output and employment, the effects among other things e.g. job insecurity. Majority of the people of Nigeria derived their income from labour. Anything that affects their job is socially disrupted and thus brings tension to the fabric of the society and also creates industrial conflicts.

As noted by David (1997), the highly educated people are people with sophisticated skills and better and more equipped to meet challenges of the competitive world. One other area of globalization is that it tends to transmit the cultural pattern of developed countries to the rest of the world. For instance, Nigerian youths have been culturally colonized. This is because they now imitate the European's consumption patterns, modes of transport, method of communication including music, without regard for the local culture. Though, it is noticed that this problem does not affect Nigerians only, it is a worldwide phenomenon. This trend would eventually lead to homogenization of economic values, thereby eliminating or reducing Nigerian economy to nothing.

Globalization gives rise to macro-economy instability that had characterised Nigerian government. This problem shows that Nigerian economic development may remain only a dream and difficult to actualise. A highly globalised and integrated financial market spreads rapidly across countries financial shocks and loss of confidence that affect exchange rate, interest rate, assets prices with the resultant effect on output and employment and ultimately adverse social effects.

It is therefore suggested by Annan (2000) that if globalization is to succeed, it must increase the life of every inhabitant of global neighbourhood without excluding Nigerians. Furthermore, for globalization to succeed, it must also deliver right no less than riches and provides social justice and equity no less than economic prosperity and enhanced communication. That is why Yakubu (1999) observes that much as we are enthused about the technological and economic wonder of globalization, we must not as Nigerians forget that vast areas of our continent still remain excluded and invisible. In spite of globalization for example, Africa is the only continent according to Yakubu (1999), in which poverty has increased since the 1970s and in which government use up to 70% of their GDP to service debts.

Economic globalization should both be driven by desire to make money. This is because profit motive rarely takes into account the poor and the disadvantage or the long term need of the planet. The global economy should be regulated and should not be dominated by corporations that recognise money as their only value. It should be noted that unregulated global economy is inherently unstable. Also an unregulated economy dominated by corporation having the desire to make profit will only increase poverty.

Finally, collective action is needed to safeguard global ethnic that will regulate globalization. Nigerian government should ensure food security for the nation rather than allowing exportation of insufficient agricultural produce, thereby bringing scarcity of food and high prices of food stuff which are unbearable to most Nigerian families upon the nation.

CHAPTER EIGHT: THE MEANING OF POLITICS

Definition

Politics is from the Greek word Polis which means 'City-state' originally concerned with the government of the Greek state. The transitive verb Politico means to administer the affairs of state, or to govern a city or state. For many people, politics solely has to do with organisation and administration of government and in that sense belongs to the politicians.

Sharfritz (1988) opines that politics is the art and science of government, the means by which the will of the community is arrived at and implemented, the activities of a government, politicians or political party. It is the pursuit and exercise of the political power necessary to make binding policy decisions for the community and to distribute patronage and other government benefits.

Politics has to do with organising the affairs of a community or a society in order to maintain law and order to preserve continued existence of a society. It is the art of ruling, controlling, directing a group of people either formally or informally appointed to enforce the law and the moral values of a given community. It can also be regarded as the instrument used by the state or a given society to enforce rules for the common good of the people and the society as a whole (Osibodu, 2004).

Ilori (1990) argues that Greek and Roman times, politics has been considered to include all the big issues that have to do with the manner of the ordering or organisation in peace and war, of the affair of societies and states. The making of the law to guide men, the distribution of resources in society, all comes under an important and necessary aspect of politics. The great aims of politics include all the aspects of how to organise or order things, and the creation of legislature and governments or magistrates to guide men and society.

According to Aristotle, man is naturally a political animal. This can be further explained to mean a situation whereby two or more people engage or are involved in political Association. It is a complex process which involves the attitude and interest of the citizens, groups and organisations. The purpose of politics, according to Aristotle, is to provide for the basic needs of life, but it continues in being for the sake of good life. It is the game of power, it has to do with the process whereby a political office seeker wooed the people he intends to serve for their mandate by presenting his manifesto to them (Asoga-Allen, 2003).

Every human community provides itself with some form of government in the first place if it is to survive, but when it has done this and organised itself, the state machinery can, and should do a great many things to make its citizens' life more worthy of living.

Politics can only bring about development in the realm of

social, economic and accelerated individual upliftment if those in politics are really committed and have sacrificed the spirit of "self" for the spirit of stateism. The economy of politics are measured by the conducive life the people of the nation live, the level of infrastructural development, the per capital income to mention a few, which are all products of prudent management.

What is needed in politics is honesty, dedication, loyalty, patriotism, commitment and determination to really serve the people. When these qualities are absent in those who rule a nation, that nation would certainly find it difficult to attain greatness. It is an obvious and conspicuous fact that a nation, whose politicians are possessed with the spirit of self, would only produce few rich and highly comfortable politicians, while the people they serve would wallow in chronic poverty.

Nigerian Politics

Politics in Nigeria is not only a dirty game but also a dangerous game. Most Nigerian politicians see politics as a do or die affair that is why a lot of credible Nigerians do not like to participate in politics. A lot of Nigerians have lost their lives as a result of participating in politics. The do or die nature of Nigerian politics was informed by the fact that politics is the most lucrative 'business' in the country. No sooner you are elected to a position than you become a millionaire. Secondly, politics in Nigeria is not seen by most Nigerian politicians as a means of serving he people but instead, they see it as a way of enriching oneself and carving out a new status or class in the society.

No wonder, you find a politician sending hired killer to one another, recruiting and maintaining thugs to oppress and suppress opponents, bribing the electorates to vote them at all cost, and using charms, invocation, and other spiritual means to subdue or eradicate their opponents.

Election in Nigeria had never reflected the will of majority, but the will of the "kabal", the few rich political figures - which constituted themselves as the kingmakers. The ascendance to the throne of any political office holder was based on the nomination by this few powerful individuals rather than by the general public or citizens. That is the more reason why after they have been sworn in, they direct their loyalty to these few individuals rather than to the general public. They take decisions and policies that favour the rich at the expense of the poor masses. They ensure that the poverty level is so high that people cannot reject the N200, N300 naira being offered to them during election to buy their conscience.

When the Election Day is approaching, you see politicians distributing money, food stuff, and other valuables to the masses to win their conscience. With ordinary N200 or a bread of N60.00, a lot of people would vote against their conscience. That shows the level of poverty in the country. The masses are unaware that by collecting money from the politicians they have sold their future. The politicians who paid money before securing your vote would not do anything for the community when they get to power; after all he paid for your service. Also, money spent to contest election, would be the first to be recovered after getting to power.

On the day of election, it has always been a thug of war. Thugs recruited by each contestant go about harassing, terrorising, bullying on the followers of opponents. Some engage themselves in fight, resulting in serious injury or death. That is the reason some people prefer to remain indoor on the day of election, to avoid being brutalized by thugs. The thugs are not limited to the youths; we have elderly ones whose profession is thuggery. They act as consultants to political office seekers/holders; they control fleet of thugs and caused catastrophe and pandemonium in the cities by their activities. They killed maimed, kidnapped, destroyed and oppressed opponents of their candidates. A typical example of such elderly thugs was Adedibu of Ibadan and Uba of Anambra. The Ibadan people would not forget in a hurry the turbulent, fearful and destructive activities of Adedibu and his gang.

At the polling stations, some dreadful thugs carry ballot box, intimidate those who are for their candidate's opponent, some are used as guards who secure a house where some unscrupulous people thumb-print ballot papers illegally for their candidates. In fact, a lot happens during election days in Nigeria. Even the security agents are not left out. Many of them are biased and work for powerful contestants. They use their gun power to intimidate and cause fear on the people in order to ensure the success of their candidates.

It becomes inevitable for the security agents to take side especially when the president or governor in power is involved, in the election. It had always been the case in Nigeria, when the incumbent president or governor is contesting with someone not in government. It must be stressed here that the idea of incumbent president or governor contesting power with an ordinary citizen is not healthy for any democracy. The president or governor controls the state machineries. In a situation like this, the state machinery would certainly work for him to ensure that he wins the election by all means.

The idea of allowing the incumbent president or governor to contest election is a great injustice in a developing country like Nigeria. This is so because the president appoints the Inspector General of Police (IGP), the Chairman of Electoral Commission, the Director General of the State Security Services (SSS) and even the head of the Army, Navy, and the Air Force. It is true that the governor presently does not control the police and the SSS, but he is chief security officer of the state. He has great influence on these agencies since their heads are members of the State Security Council. In essence, to make an ordinary citizen to contest election with the incumbent president or governor in a country like Nigeria is a great risk and deadly.

The leaders that emerge in most cases are those forced on the people not the ones elected by them, thus no leader seem to see himself responsible to the citizen or people. The kind of democracy being practiced by Nigerians is the type that could be called adulterated and nominative democracy, not pure one. For example, a situation whereby an election is rigged to produce an unpopular candidate at the expense of popular candidate cannot be called democracy. An election which the results represent the interest of the people is the type that could be linked to democracy. Democracy is a game of number, majority always carry the votes, and not minority as it is the case in Nigeria.

The common saying of the politician is that they are into politics to serve their people, but this is not correct. People are into politics in Nigeria to serve them. That is why it is difficult for the nation to develop. No leader seems to have the interest of the masses and that the nation at heart. Everyone thinks about what they can benefit from Nigeria not what they can contribute to make Nigeria great. After they have accumulated wealth, they travel abroad and established themselves there, forgetting that those advanced countries they travelled to often and often were developed by the people of those countries.

Nigerian Politics and the Issue of Development

In a democratic setting, politics brings about development to the society. That is where the rules of the game are followed and the politicians are determined to sacrifice the spirit of self for that of the nation. For politics to bring about development politicians must render selfless service and shun corruption. It is painful that this has not been so in Nigeria. Those who are opportune to rule the nation are only interested in self-aggrandizement rather than national greatness. The corruptive behaviour of most past leaders was so pronounced that at the end of their tenure, they were richer than the nation they ruled. That is, they command billions of naira, dollar and pound sterling while the nation they ruled remains stagnant, without any evidence of development.

Politics has developed America, United Kingdom, France to mention a few, but as far as Nigeria is concerned, there was nothing to show as meaningful development on the part of the nation. The only thing that is conspicuous is individuals who were as poor as church rat hitherto, but have emerged as millionaires and billionaires after holding a political office for a period of just four years. Despite the wealth or resources that abound in this nation, those who are not in politics are wallowing in poverty and penury.

All segments of the national development were grounded. With the number of years of independence, Nigeria cannot boast of regular supply of electricity, no good roads, no good hospitals, education is totally paralysed by incessant strikes of the workers in the sector as a result of poor condition of service and poor funding of education generally. No sector of the nation could be said to have developed. The only things that are developing are individual politicians who built mansions, command chains of expensive cars/jeeps and robust bank accounts both at home and abroad.

Except we want to deceive ourselves, politics/politicians have failed the nation. The worst part is the issue of tribal politics that has led to rotation of presidency and some vital posts in politics. This has not helped the nation at all. Instead, it had allowed mediocre to be presented as president of the Federal Republic of Nigeria. A lot of Commanders-in-Chief of Federal Republic of Nigeria could not command anything except poverty and suffering. If it is necessary for certain posts to be rotated among the various ethnic groups or geographical zones, only the best candidates should have been presented and accepted for such positions, not someone who lack ability to preside over a town being made a president over the whole country.

As far as the state of the nation is concerned today, only the politicians and their business associates could say it is well with the country. It is so because they always justify it that all is well with Nigeria, that Nigerians are not poor despite the World Bank rating that most Nigerians live on less than $1 dollar per day. That is living below poverty line.

Nigerians except the politicians and their business associates have been enslaved economically by the politicians. Many would not agree to this fact because for one to realise this depends so much on individual's ability to analyse situations. It is no more news that the bulk of the nation's resources are shared by politicians. Civil servants are poorly paid but the politicians' salaries are beyond imagination. The most surprising thing is that politicians in Nigeria have no conscience. What is major human in human being is the ability to think rationally and to conscientiously feel what is right and what is wrong. The Local Government Councillor who is the least politician in Nigeria and with academic qualification of school certificate, earns higher than a university professor who likely have trained the president, governors and ministers. The 2009 rating of Transparency International shows that Nigerian politicians are the highest paid politicians in the world and Nigerian workers are the most poorly paid workers in the world.

Whenever the workers asked for increase in wages, they silent them down, they talk to them like slaves that only deserve his daily food, not necessarily balanced diet but something just to be given to him to keep him alive not to make him fat. Those who are not working with the government are totally forgotten as if they are not part of the nation. They are not benefiting anything rather; they are forced to pay taxes to the government. Both the local, state and federal government agents are always on the people's neck asking for one levy or another. If not for these agents, one would have doubted if actually there is government in most areas of the nation. In most part of Nigeria, everyone is the provider of borehole, electricity, health and even security. Then, what are the functions of the government to the people? Some people claimed that the nation is too large, that it should not be compared with other nations, but the issue of largeness should not be talked about at all, because it is irrelevant. Just as the nation is large so also it is endowed with abundant natural resources.

A lot of avenue of government are wasteful as they are not performing any role to the society. Take for example, the local government councils in Nigeria. A lot of allocations are being given to them on quarterly basis, but apart from paying their staff salaries, nothing else is being done. The allocations are shared by politicians. It is expected that the local government should be able to repair local roads, if it is to fill the pot holes, make gutters and even dig boreholes for rural areas to enable them get clean water to drink, but none of these is being done, still, we refer to them as local government. With the level of poverty in Nigeria today, local government is an avenue of waste. Any government that is not performing any function to the society is not a government.

The situation of Nigeria is getting worse on daily basis, year-in-year-out the situation is getting worse. For example, the situation of Nigeria four years ago was better than that of three years ago, that of three years ago was better than that of two years ago; that of two years ago was better than last year, last year was better than this year. Who knows how Nigeria would be in the next five years? There is no doubt that if the ruler-ship of Nigeria still continues to be in the hands of these crops of politicians, everyone would be tired and fed up with Nigeria. In essence, the future of Nigeria is very bleak and unsafe in the hands of these unscrupulous politicians. Even now everyone is tired with unfulfilled promises. One president would come and tell you, he has 9 point agenda; another one would tell you 16 point agenda and so on and so forth. All these are mere paper work and lip services. Nigerians want to see a honest leader, a great and pragmatic achiever, not a looter and mediocre who cannot perform. Not a leader whose idea centres on how to add more suffering to the ones Nigerians are already going through.

Essential products like cement, salt, rice to mention a few are contracted to single or few Nigerians to import from abroad, these few Nigerians control the destinies of all other Nigerians and make life better for them by charging exorbitant amount on these products. The government cannot call them to order because they are members of the kabals that rule the nation.

The problem of electricity remains unsolved despite the billions of naira injected into it because the kabals are responsible for importing generators. Also, the refineries can never work properly because the kabals are responsible for the importation of petroleum. They say Nigerians engage in smuggling, why wouldn't they do so when people in the neighbouring countries, who do not even have any tangible resources, enjoy goods at cheaper prices than Nigerians who have all the resources in heaven and earth? Or how would you explain the high import duties charged by Nigerian Ports? Even the World Bank Commented in 2009 that one of the problems facing Nigerian economy is that Nigerian Ports charge too much import duties and too much items were banned from entering the country.

Except, God liberates Nigerians from the slavery which fellow Nigerians have pushed them into, the future of Nigerians is bleak and uncertain. The masses have made a lot of sacrifice in the past hoping that things were going to be alright but all to no avail. It is the masses that are object of sacrifice. Those in politics have more than enough. What they accumulate is enough to sustain them and their future generations. A lot of people have died waiting for a better day. A lot would still die because the better day may not come during the time of these politicians. The worst part is that those who are old among the politicians have started to replace themselves with their children who also toe the line of their fathers. The deregulation policy being pursued by the government is a design by the kabal to push the Nigerian masses more into slavery or to add to their suffering. Venezuela an oil producing country like Nigeria organized their economy in such a way that $1.2 dollar is used to fuel a car. That is a full tank of car costs $1.2 dollars. According to the Venezuela ambassador in Nigeria, Mr. Enrique, deregulation of the oil sector is tantamount to Nigerians giving their economy to the foreigner to control. He advised Nigerians to look inward for solution to their problems rather than outward. According to him, Venezuela had twelve (12) functional refineries, education is not only free up to university level but the university students are fed thrice a day (The Punch, 2009). The country Venezuela has twenty two thousand (22,000) doctors; these doctors visit people at home to treat.

Only low intelligent people would be hoping for a better day from the way the nation is going now. Though in the perspective of religion, one may be looking unto God for his intervention. Certainly, the boat of Nigeria is in bad hands. The nation is not heading towards development but retrogression. People hate the truth but cherish lies. When you say all is well with Nigeria, Nigeria is the giant of Africa, those in government would see you as a good Nigerian. But when you say openly that Nigeria is in trouble, people are dying as a result of hardship, or point out the wrongdoing of the politicians, you become an enemy of the people. They would tag you an unpatriotic citizen. When any foreign government criticises the government for bad administration, is accused of talking rubbish. President Obama of United States visited Ghana in Africa in 2009, because Ghana was seen as a model of democracy in West Africa. He spoke much of corruption (both economic and political), also he spoke of purposeful government that could move a nation forward. Most of what he said is things that affect Nigeria.

Likewise, Mrs. Rawlings, the Secretary for Foreign Affairs, United States of America, visited Nigeria and some African countries, and pointed out the wrong doings associated with governance in Nigeria. Instead of government to accept this in good faith and amend their ways, they condemned what the

U.S government said and started to defend themselves that all were in order, no problem with Nigeria. Abdulkareem, a Nigerian musician, some years ago, sang a song in Pidgin English that "Nigeria jagajaga, everything scarter scarter, poor man dey suffer suffer everything scarter scarter". That was the time Chief Olusegun Obasanjo was president of the Federal Republic of Nigeria. Obasanjo was so furious that he referred to the parents of Abdulkareem as being Jagajaga. Assuming Abdulkareem had sang that Nigeria is the best country to be in the world, Obasanjo would have invited him for a handshake if not giving him cash.

Another dimension to the issue of tribal politics that is acting as an impediment or bottleneck to the development of the nation is the cultural differences of the various ethnic groups. For example, there is a particular major ethnic group that does not believe in tomorrow. That is, whatever money that is in the treasury today should be spent, if there is no money tomorrow, they have to borrow. This culture can never allow the nation to develop. As long as it continues, the nation would remain stagnant and the ordinary people would continue to suffer. This is a basic fact because whatever is accumulated in terms of cash when a president from prudent tribe mounted the throne would soon be wasted as soon as somebody from "eat all", spend all tribe receive the mantle of leadership and before you know it, the nation is in debt again.

This issue of reckless or wasteful spending of one particular ethnic group from one geographical zone is a crucial one that

Nigerians generally need to handle with all seriousness if actually we intend to attain greatness one day as we speculate. Right thinking Nigerians feel that except this tribe has an attitudinal change the nation would forever remain poor and underdeveloped. If you go into history, more people from the north have ruled the nation than those from the south. Except General Yakubu Gowon whose tenure as the military head of state brought an unprecedented progress to the nation, much cannot be said of the others like Shagari, Babangida, Abacha, Abdulkareem and even with Yar Adua, going by the trend of things, much may not happen.

General Buhari, may be, would have made a difference like Yakubu Gowon because the little time he spent as military head of state, he initiated a great revolution aimed at restoring normalcy and put Nigeria on path of development, but his administration was short-lived as he was overthrown by General Ibrahim Badamasi Babangida and his group. Whether people like this fact or not, it is a basic truth that must be said. This is 21st Century, more than 49 years of Nigerian independence. Still, Nigeria has been made lame and incapacitated by unscrupulous rulers. Obasanjo handed over government to Yar Adua, just about two years and some months ago. One of the few successes recorded by Obasanjo's regime was the debt forgiveness/payment of Nigerian debts. As at today, debt has started to pile up under the Yar Adua's government. The question is how long are we going to continue this? It is based on this serious predicament that one could support other Nigerians calling for the splitting of this nation into more countries or regions in line with the major ethnic groups. The Hausa land is large enough to form two countries, the middle belt, a country and the Igbo land or south south.

Let each ethnic group be ruled by her indigene, if the leader likes, he should rule well and ensure good condition of living for his people or allowing his people to be begging for alms all over as a result of poverty. If this is the only way development could come to this part of the world, it then becomes pertinent and inevitable to split. There is no glory in being united in poverty. The reason why this has to be executed in time is the fact that this nation cannot continue like this for long. It is better to do this in peace than to allow it done through war that could claim innocent lives and properties.

Unity may only stand for ever where all the united people are subjected to the same condition, living the same standard, and there is transparency, accountability, probity, justice, fairness and equity. Where there are various standards, some are stinking rich by embezzling what belongs to the public and other lived an impoverished, retched, poor and unworthy life, the issue of unity would not last long because some people would not mind to die instead of allowing fake unity to stand. Unity is known to bring about progress, stability and greatness e.g. United States of America; this could be due to the commitment, dedication, patriotism and loyalty of Americans. It was not by accident. Anything that does not bring the above is fake unity.

People talk of constitution review, the question is what is wrong with the existing constitution? Is it the constitution that is making people corrupt or rigging election? Or commit all sorts of atrocities going on in the country? If the constitution is amended ten times in a year, the story would still be the same. There is nothing wrong with the constitution but the people that implement the constitution. It is the people that need attitudinal change to make the constitution work. Using a whole one billion naira or more to amend the constitution is a colossal waste of the nation's resources.

Also, the rebranding of Nigeria being embarked upon by Professor Dora Akunyili, the Nigerian Minister for Information, is seen by most rational thinking Nigerians as a mere political propaganda that cannot yield any meaningful result. Even, if you call Nigerians excellent people when they are not, what importance would that be? Is that not a mere window display? It is like painting a tomb full of human bones white. It would appear white to whoever sees it but inside it is full of human bones. Calling Nigeria a great nation is a mere appellation. Is Nigeria really great when electricity is not functioning, no good roads, no pipe borne water, no good hospital and so on and so forth. Perhaps, it is because millions of Nigerian graduates are jobless, workers (civil servants) and the masses generally are groaning in poverty that made Nigeria a great nation. Might be Professor Dora Akunyili was being sighted because of her positions as former National Foods and Drugs Administration and Control's (NAFDAC)

Director for five years and a Minister for Information. She couldn't remember the true picture of Nigeria, unlike when she was a lecturer earning poor salary in the campus.

I could not see any difference between the national rebirth launched by Obasanjo's government that did not change anything and her rebranding. Nigerians have been deceived enough. No propaganda would fascinate anyone any longer. What Nigerians need is attitudinal change and for that to happen, it must come from the top. If our leaders change their attitude today, the followers would have no alternative than to emulate. Any call for a change of attitude that is targeted at the masses when the leaders have not changed will never achieve any result. In fact, it is a child's play; it cannot be of any effect.

A lot of government agencies could not achieve their objectives because the government that set them up is not a clean government and there is no way they could perform without implicating those in government or their associates. For example, the Independent Corrupt Practices Commission (ICPC) and the Economic Financial Crimes Commission (EFCC) set up by the Federal Government has not and cannot win corruption battle because if they are to really fight corruption, a lot of those in government or past leaders would have to answer questions on their past and present activities. Thus, it seems only those who have one score or the other to settle with the government or their political opponents are being investigated.

Ideally, whoever would fight corruption and win the battle in Nigeria must be a person or persons with clean hands, not people who have corruptly enriched themselves and are now having billions of naira. If corrupt people champion the crusade against corruption, no one would take them serious. Rather, people would look at them as hypocrites who preached that stealing is bad after they have stolen enough for themselves and their families.

The way corrupt people are treated in Nigeria could encourage corruption. When a person is accused for embezzling billions of naira and is arrested, he employs the services of a lawyer who seeks his bail. After his bail, he becomes a free person; he begins to enjoy his ill-gotten wealth. If at all there is judgement at the end, it may take years, and at the end they are imprisoned just for few months or years or the known property are forfeited to the government, while he enjoys the ones kept secret. Those who are caught in armed robbery are to die by firing squad. The point here is that stealing is stealing whether it is committed by arm or by pen.

In the history of the nation (Nigeria) no armed robber has been able to rob anyone or bank of one billion naira, but we have found individuals that have robbed the nation of more than ten (10) billion naira. If it is so, is it not wrong to execute somebody who stole in millions and set free someone who stole in billions? It is true that armed robbers kill sometimes in an attempt to carry out their actions but one must not forget that the pen robbers also kill more than the armed robbers. For example, when billions are stolen from the economy of any nation, one could imagine the effect on the masses. During the tenure of some past rulers in Nigeria, many children died of diseases related to lack of balanced diet (kwashiorkor). A lot of parents were retrenched from their work places and those in service were paid like slaves, that they could not feed their families. This was true of the time of Shagari, Babangida and Abacha.

Nigerians were subjected to all sorts of economic measures e.g. devaluation of currency (DC), Structural Adjustment Programme (SAP), Cutting of Government Spending (CGS), to mention a few. All these economic adjustment programmes did not bring any success on the economy of the nation, rather, the masses only suffered for nothing. When Nigerian government adopts any economic adjustment programme, it is the welfare of the masses that would suffer. The spending of government or their allocations would still remain intact. Some adjustment programme are embarked upon to enable those leaders have enough to steal from the treasury.

In conclusion, the type of politics played in Nigeria vis-a-vis the mentality and idiosyncrasy of the politicians cannot bring about development, rather, it is a politics of corruption and dishonesty that is capable of stagnating the progress and economic development of the nation. When such politics go for a long time it would reach a climax, saturated point and if not properly handled, it will result into chaos and anarchy because the oppressed would be ready to die and they would resist and checkmate the activities of the tyrants, oppressors and self-centred individuals that rule them. Though, this may be bloody, at the end of it a new society, new order and legitimate authority would emerge.

CHAPTER NINE: NIGERIA DEMOCRACY AND RELIGION

The Concept of Religion

The English word religion has been in use since the 13th century, loaned from Anglo-French religrun (11th century), ultimately from the Latin religio, "reverence for God or the gods, careful ponderin of divine things, piety, the res divinance". The ultimate origins of Latin religio are obscure. It is usually accepted to derive from Ligare "bind connect", likely from a prefix re-ligare, i.e. re (again) + Ligare or "to connect". The interpretation is favoured by modern scholars such as Tom Harpur and Joseph Campbell, but was made prominent by St. Augustine, following the interpretation of Lactantius.

A religion can also be described as a set of stories, symbols, beliefs and practices, often with a supernatural quality that gives meaning to the practitioner's experiences of life to reference to an ultimate power or reality. It may be expressed through prayer, ritual, meditation, music and art, among other things. It may focus on specific supernatural, metaphysical and moral claims about reality (the cosmos and human nature which may yield a set of religious laws, ethics and a particular lifestyle. Religion also encompasses ancestral or cultural traditions, writings, history and mythology as well as personal faith and religious experience.

The term "religion" refers to both the personal practices

related to communal faith and to group rituals and communications stemming from shared convictions, and it entails specific behaviours respectively.

The development of religion has taken many forms in various cultures. It considers psychological and social roots, along with origins and historical development. In the frame of western religious thought, religions present a common quality, the "hallmark of patriarchal religious thoughts", the division of world in two comprehensive domains, one sacred and other profane. Religion is often described as a communal system for the coherence of belief focusing on a system of thought, unseen being, person or object, that is considered to be supernatural, sacred, divine or of the highest truth. Moral codes, practices, values, institutions, tradition, rituals and scriptures are often traditionally associated with the core belief and these may have some overlap with concepts in secular philosophy. Religion is also often described as a "way of life" or a life stance.

Religion according to Idowu (1962) as quoted in Opajobi (1999) is a difficult topic to handle whether we are considering its root meaning, its connotation, its origin or its definition. In addition, Stark (1987) also expressed that the most difficult problem facing sociologists of religion has been to define this subject matter. However, Leuba has collected forty eight definitions of religion (Anyaocha, 1993).

Olayinka (1999) stated that religion unlike other disciplines like music, Geography, History, Mathematics, Chemistry, it is difficult to give a satisfactory and universal definition of the term. Professor Leuba after being given forty eight definitions and adding two of his own still felt unsatisfied. Generally speaking, scholars of different opinions in giving an acceptable definition of religion, according to Olayiwola (1995) scholars tend to define religion either very narrowly or too broadly that the term looses all significance. It is also misleading to think of religion as a code of ethics or of moral since there are people who can reject all religions and still maintain high moral and ethical standards. Belief in a religion or loyalty to a particular faith is no guarantee against immoral or unethical behaviour.

According to African encyclopaedia (1994) as quoted by Olayiwola (1999), "religion includes beliefs from all parts of the world about goals", some religion like Christianity and Islam teach that there is only one God. In all religious teaching however, it is believed that God(s) have power over all things, which are beyond the control of man. This is explained further that man cannot only ask for good things and try to demand them from God by doing what they believe the God(s) want.

Religion is the belief about the divine supernatural being (God). According to Christian religion, it is believed that God created the heaven and earth and all that are in it, and that God created man (human beings) specifically to be serving and worshipping him. All religions that have to do with God preach morality, good value, virtues and peaceful co-existence. Religion gives meaning and hope to human existence, and the doctrines of most religion if adhered to are capable of ensuring an egalitarian society. Societies where people fear God, keep his commandments, and make the word of God the standard of their behaviour.

The word of God is supposed to be the standard by which the Christians and Muslims measure themselves, if actually they are in faith. Doing the right thing and guiding themselves against wrong doings and correcting their actions where they have fallen short of the standard. Any religion that has to do with God must inculcate honesty, obedience, good virtue, morality, loyalty and patriotism. That is why religion is an important subject in the school curriculum both at the primary and secondary school levels. The rationality of religion goes beyond preparing oneself or preparing people for the kingdom of heaven, but also it tends to make a prospective individual, a worthy member of the society who lives a life of an achiever, righteous and trustworthiness.

The role of religion in the society cannot be over-emphasized. It helps to mould human minds by removing the natural instincts that are capable of extincting the society. In Christian religion, we read in the Holy Bible in the Book of Genesis chapter 6 verses 5 - 6 that God regretted that he created man because the imagination of man's heart is completely evil. From this verse one could adduce that naturally man has an evil instinct and is capable of doing evil. If not for religion, it would be difficult for man to trust man. Even, the word of God made us understand that the heart of man is evil, who can understand it.

Religion helps to some extent to remove the abnormality in a man who has given himself or his life to God. Before the advent of Christianity and Islamic religion, people already had religion in Nigeria like many other African countries. This religion is referred to as traditional religion. People believe in God and try to reach him through lesser gods. They worship idols. There were Dos and Don'ts, taboos, norms, values which each society formulated and perpetrated. In the olden days, there were no human police; the Gods were there to arrest whoever acted contrary to the rules and regulations of the society.

Unlike the situation in Christian and Islamic religion where people swear falsely, or do what is against the society and go scot-free, anyone who swears falsely in those days would receive the result in a matter of days. There were some fearful gods such as Sango, Ogun, Aiyelala to mention a few. You don't joke with these gods when it comes to establishing the fact of a case or arresting the offender. These gods pronounced instant judgement and this made people in traditional society to resist or reluctant to do evil because they do not want to face unfavourable consequences that would accompany their uncompromising or unruly behaviour.

These gods helped to enforce obedience to the societal rules and regulations and serve as the security agents or incorruptible judge. The latter introduced religions,

Christianity and Islam are religions in which God's mercies are enlarged and God allows an evil doer a long rope for him to change. The Holy Bible made us understand that God is slow to anger. The first world was destroyed with water in annoyance by God and since that time God had promised not to destroy the world again irrespective of what man has done. Though judgement would surely come to every man according to his work but not as immediate as to serve as deterrent to others. That is the reason why today, most of our past and present leaders underestimate God. After swearing with the Holy Bible or Qur'an, they do contrary to their oath, and betray the people that brought them to power.

One percent (1%) love of Nigeria is not in them, they are only attracted to Nigeria because of what they intend to benefit from it. They have no plan for Nigeria's future. In fact, they are not concerned about what becomes of Nigeria; they are only concerned about themselves and immediate members of their families. In an attempt to grab what belongs to the public and corner it into their purse, they are ready to do anything. Human lives to them are nothing, but still they bear Christian names and Arabic names.

The Role of Religion in Nigerian Politics

It is not an exaggeration to say that Nigeria is one of the most religious nations of the world. Churches and mosques are found in all nooks and crannies of the country. There is rarely any village where a church or mosque is not found. In the cities, you found churches all about. There are streets with more than find churches, likewise mosques. But the irony of it is that the impact that the religion is expected to have on the people are completely absent in most Nigerians. In fact, the state of religion in Nigeria made one understand that one may be religious and not Christian or Muslim.

The disciples of Jesus Christ were called Christians in Antioch not because they prayed, or performed miracles but simply because they were Christ-like in their behaviours. The churches are filled up with people who have one problem or the other, people who want miracle, who want to be rich and want breakthrough, but those who really love God are very few. They carry along all the old ways of life, they lie, they steal, they kill, they covet, and they conspire to mention a few. The Christian religion or Islamic religion that they profess has not taken anything from them. That is, they are not born again, the love of the world or flesh has eaten up most of them. The kingdom of God which the Bible says should be sought first and all other things which include wealth, long life, greatness power and so on and so forth would be added are now taken as second while what God calls additions are now the first that the people pursue.

Nobody, I repeat nobody seems to be thinking about the kingdom of God. Rather, people think of the worldly things. The fear of God is completely absent in them no wonder just as the church and mosque increases in Nigeria, the crime rate also increases. Religion has no meaning again; people only go to church and mosque because they need one thing or the other. Even the armed robbers go to church/mosque to ask for protection from being caught. Repentant Christians/Muslims are very rare to come by. Anyone who mistakenly enters into business with someone because he or she attends church or mosque regularly most of the time, regret such contract or agreement.

The worst part is that people use the name of Jesus/Muhammad to commit all sorts of atrocity. When it comes to money matter, people are ready to swear falsely with the Holy Bible/Quran, because people swear falsely and go scot free. No one seems to fear God again. Apart from the unbeliever mere church goers, you see fake pastors who obtained power from Satan and start to deceive people by performing all sorts of miracles. The only two ways approved by the Holy Bible as a pre-requisite to signs and wonders are through prayer and fasting. But surprisingly you see pastors who neither fasted nor prayed performing miracles.

A lot of people who do not want to go to the herbalist end up in the hands of a herbalist who disguised to be a pastor. When some so called men of God speak, one start wondering whether they are really born again, even among some highly placed men of God. Many have given up the work that Jesus called them to do. The love of money has eroded their faith in God. Instead of preaching the word of God, they preach money. Most of them see themselves as successful because of the amount of billions of naira and hard currencies they have in banks, the wealth accumulated instead of the number of souls won for God.

In a corrupt society like Nigeria, real men of God have significant role to play to effect attitudinal change. If all the men of God should speak with one voice, no politician would rule the nation the way he or she likes. Many of the men of God, even the highly placed ones have lost focus, all their interest is how to amass wealth instead of telling the politicians the truth; they worship and praise them so as to receive financial benefits. You see a highly placed man of God rejoicing because a highly placed politician who has failed the nation, and plunged the masses into poverty and untold suffering as a result of his corrupt practices, has visited him or come to worship in his church.

The preaching in most churches/mosques today are not the type that can make people repent from their evil ways rather it is the type that would make people go deeper into unrighteousness. For example, no matter how religious and faithful a man is, he cannot be recognised in the church today except he has money. And even, if a person is an armed robber or a fraud star, provided he is rich and also support the church with money regularly, most pastors would carry him like king. The questions is that, is it the religion based on money that the Lord Jesus handed over to Nigerian pastors? Or where did they read that Jesus was after worldly things as they are doing today?

Jesus tells us that those who labour and are heavy laden should come on to him that he would give them rest. But as it is today, can the poor find rest in the church again? Has not many pastors turned the churches to where more loads are added to those who are heavy laden, thereby making their loads extraordinarily heavy? Or how do you explain a situation whereby the pastor is commanding millions and a lot of members of his church cannot boast of one good square meal a day?

In Nigeria today, some men of God collect money before they pray for people, give preferential treatment to the rich members of the church, and pursue accumulation of wealth like unbelievers. There is nothing bad in pastor becoming rich, but it has to be in Godly way, not through self wisdom or using the name of Jesus to exploit the members or the public. We have read and heard a situation where a church member stole millions of naira in his place of work and brought it to the church and the pastor received it without questioning him on where he got the money. It took frantic effort of the security agents to recover the money from the church when the employer discovered the theft and reported the case to the police.

Most of the crusades or programmes held in some churches are not focused and targeted towards the salvation of human souls or winning souls for Christ, rather, they are targeted towards collection of offerings. In essence, not only politicians failed the nation, even many men of God have failed God and the nation, as their emphasis is no longer the kingdom of God but on acquisition of wealth. That is the reason why everyone wants to own a church, that is, to make money. Church is now a business venture where the name of God is used to make money and become stinking rich. One could see why the society is full of corrupt and evil minded people. Money has been lifted above God, thus, encouraging all the immoralities. That is why the idea of asking pastors/Imam to pay tax by some state governors is highly welcomed.

In another dimension, the issue of religion in Nigeria today deserves special attention. It is true that no religion preaches violence, but the adherents of some religion had turned their religion to an instrument of violence, killing and maiming innocent people in some part of Nigeria. Millions of lives have been wasted and properties worth billions of naira have been destroyed in the name of religion. The nation's leader had not seen any need to take a drastic step against those who kill in the name of religion and prevent future occurrence. If somebody from influential family had been killed, things would have changed, but because there is no regard for lives of the poor masses, people only pay lip services to the termination of innocent lives.

Some religious leaders are so ungodly and deceitful in their message to their followers. For example, how would someone continue to tell his supporters that if they died in the course of fighting for God, they would go to heaven. Which heaven would such people go to? Is God so lazy that He requires human beings that he created to fight for him? God is the most powerful, He creates and He has power to destroy. If He feels like doing so, He does not require anyone to fight for Him. And if actually, God wants people to fight for Him in either Christianity or Islam, the Pastor/Imam who led the congregation should be the one to be at the front of the fight. But, this has never been the case, instead the fools, people with low intelligence are pushed into such fight, while the Imam/keep his children at home with his wives, enjoying. Does it mean, he does not want to go to al-Jana?

It is high time we talk against the way innocent lives of Yorubas and Igbos and their properties are being wasted in the northern part of Nigeria in the name of religion. The most annoying thing is that some of these religious crises emerged out of flimsy excuses. For example, a newspaper in Spain carried or portrayed a prophet in Islam in a wrong way that was what led to the killing of thousands of Nigerians residing in the northern part of Nigeria and their properties destroyed. Boko Haram crises in Bauchi, Kano and some northern cities would have resulted into mass termination of innocent lives, but for the quick intervention of President Yar Adua who deployed mobile police men and the military to the area. Still, thousands of Nigerians including some police officers lost their lives and properties worth millions of naira were destroyed.

During the first and second tenures of Chief Olusegun Obasanjo as civillian president, some Governors in the northern part introduced sharia in their states. Nobody was allowed to drink or sell alcoholic drink. But the money generated from VAT in other states where alcoholic drinks are sold was shared to all the states including sharia states and the governors of those states collected the money. Each time the people have ethnic or political scores to settle, they result to religion. That is, they carry it out in the name of religion. It is high time the leaders of the nation find a lasting solution to the issue of religion. Ideally, religion should be for peace, holiness, unity and progress, no religion preaches killing and destruction of human properties.

Nigeria is a secular state, the constitution of the Federal Republic of Nigeria does not uphold any religion above the other, that is why it emphasises that as a citizen you must respect the religion of others. No one has its constitutional right to force his religion on the other. Adherence to any religion should be based on individual interest and conviction. It is a good thing to serve God but still, in a secular state, it is not uncommon to see people who do not even believe in any religion, and they have right to live. God has power to fight for himself in any situation or circumstances. Any God that requires people to fight for him is not God but manmade. The issue of religious crisis is capable of causing disunity and regional war, if not checked.

In conclusion, anyone who claims to be religious should exhibit and display good virtues, morality, love, affection and Godliness in his character towards all people. Wherever he finds himself he should use his religion to promote the social, economic and political development of Nigeria by respecting the constitution and showing commitment, loyalty, dedication and patriotism to the nation.

CHAPTER TEN: NIGERIA DEMOCRACY AND THE MILITARY

Introduction

When we talk of military in this chapter, we mean the Nigerian Army, the Nigerian Air Force and the Naval Force. The military establishment is an essential aspect of any nation. No nation can stand peacefully and maintain its dignity and sovereignty without putting in place a strong, sophisticated and formidable army. The military is an indispensable entity of any nation. Without the military, the nation stands the risk of foreign or external attack, interference and encroachment to her territory by foreign countries, constant attack, defeat and imposition of hegemony by superior country. It is true that international laws make provision for the sovereignty of every independent nation but that is not a guarantee for any nation not to be attacked as we have seen in the past where a stronger nation attacked the weaker one. For example, the case of Russia attacks on Georgia in 2008.

The military of any nation symbolises its strength, and a nation with powerful and sophisticated standing military would be respected among the Committee of Nations. Apart from the external forces being prevented from attacking the nation, there is need to keep the nation together, that is to prevent civil strife or internal disorder. In the light of the above, it is obvious that the task performed by the military of any nation is very enormous and highly demanding.

Functions of the Military in Nigeria

The essential functions performed by the Nigerian Military include:

1.　　To defend the nation against external/ foreign attack;
2.　　To defend the sovereignty of the nation;
3.　　To maintain the nation's territorial integrity;
4.　　To fight war when its declared by the lawful authority;
5.　　To ensure that democracy thrives in the country;
6.　　To parade during important national events e.g. independent day, Army day and so on and so forth;
7.　　To participate in the maintenance of peace in any part of the world when the need arises.

The Nigerian military have participated in the restoration of peace in any troubled part of Africa and the world in general. Outside the legitimate functions stated above, the Nigerian military had at one time or the other delved into governance by overthrowing the legitimate government in Nigeria. However, the Nigerian military did not act on a vacuum; they acted based on the crying of the people over bad governance and misrule of those elected to rule the nation. After the coup, one would expect the military to organise an election and hand over government to the democratically elected people, but this was not so. Instead, they started to rule the nation, using decrees.

Each time there was military coup in the past, people jubilated hoping that they would have good government and an improved standard of living, but at the end, what the people got was frustration worse than those they overthrew. At a stage, it was no longer the matter of military taking over government from the democratically elected government but military taking over government from military. This was after it had become clearer that those that took over government from the civilians did so to enrich and protect their personal interest rather than the interest of the impoverished masses. The confidence that the people had in the military that they would restore good government was a fiasco. People started to sing a new song that both the military and civilians are corrupt and lack the interest of the nation in their hearts.

The Nigerian military are very famous in international community for their role in ensuring world peace but at home, they have not been able to influence good governance. In Ghana, the people are enjoying good governance due to the role played by their military. In West Africa, Ghana had been recognised as the best democratic nation. That was the reason why Obama visited Ghana in West Africa immediately after his inauguration and swearing in. This generated a lot of hullabaloo in Nigeria because it was expected by our politicians that if Obama would visit any country in Africa, it should be Nigeria. However, the outside world, especially nations with advanced democracy like USA does not see Nigeria from the perspective of Nigerian politicians who see nothing wrong with the governance in Nigeria.

In the speech of President Obama, delivered in Ghana, it was clear that US was unhappy about the state of corruption which had affected all segments and strata of the nation's life in Nigeria. He frowned particularly on Nigeria's inability to conduct a free and fair election, poor state of education,, unemployment, poor health and poverty among the masses. Mrs. Rawlings, the US Secretary of State repeated the same thing when she visited Nigeria in 2009 and advised Nigerian government to be transparent and shun corruption, also to ensure that results of elections in Nigeria reflect the interest of the people.

The feeling of Nigerian politicians is that democracy has come to stay, that the military will never intervene or seize the government by force again. To ensure that it is so, the leaders' right from Obasanjo have been trying to satisfy the military by seeing to their needs, forgetting that members of the military have extended families some that are very poor and retched. In essence, rather than the erroneous feelings of the leaders that if the military are well taken care of, they would not stage coup to topple the government, the only thing that can keep the military out of staging coup is good governance. Bad government would continue to warrant people's condemnation and outcry, and when this continues for some time, the military like before would have a ground to seize power. It is not a question of whether they are messiah or not.

Nigerian Democracy and the Police

The police are highly essential and most indispensable to any government. This is due to the fact that the two most significant and basic duties of any government are the maintenance of law and order and the preservation of lives and properties. The government agency for carrying out this function is the police. Without the police, it would be difficult if not impossible to maintain the law.

Functions of the Nigerian Police

According to Onibonoje (1959), the functions of the Nigerian police include:

a.   To maintain law and order;

b.   To preserve lives and properties, in order to do these, it is the duty of the police;

c.   To prevent people from committing crimes;

d.   To detect crime, if it has been committed;

e.   To arrest the offenders and bring them to the law courts for trial;

f.   at times, the police may suspect a person and arrest him or her, this is one of the ways of preventing the commission of crimes

g.   It is the duty of the police to enforce the laws, rules and court orders.

The Nigeria Police, for many years was under-funded. The men were poorly paid and the condition of service was nothing to write home about. Also, the equipment needed for effective policing was and are still lacking. Despite these, people's expectations from the Nigerian police is very high especially in the recent years where criminal activities have greatly multiplied due to unemployment resulting from bad or corrupt governments of the nation.

In present days, the work of the Nigerian police or policemen is becoming more tedious, this is so because economic hardship had given birth to all sorts of atrocities in the society. The worst is the issue of armed robbery; the robbers in recent years, carrying sophisticated weapons superior in all ways to those of the police. A lot of policemen have lost their lives in hands of armed robbers. In fact, policing is one of the dangerous jobs in Nigeria, if not the most dangerous now.

Nigerian politicians have the erroneous belief that increasing the number of policemen would solve the problem of criminality in Nigeria. But events have proved that even if you turn all Nigerians to policemen, that would not eradicate criminal activities. People take to crime mostly when they are frustrated and find it difficult to cope with life. The case of Nigeria is very conspicuous, everyone knows that the resources of the nation are enough to make every Nigerian have a fair share, that is, to live comfortably and enjoy good standard of living. But reverse seems to be the case because few individuals corner the wealth of the nation to themselves and accumulate wealth at the expense of the masses.

The Nigerian police seem to be the victim of bad and corrupt government in Nigeria because criminals are found everywhere; everyone wants to make it big by all means. One would expect the government to address the causes of crimes but instead, it is prevention that is being emphasized. It must be stressed here that except something is done urgently to arrest the rate of unemployment in Nigeria, the entire citizen would be in danger. No amount of recruitment into the police would stop crime but good government would do.

Nigeria should be made a land of equal opportunity for all, not a land where those who got their money through corrupt means dominate the other citizens. The present situation of Nigeria, that is, the way the country's economy is being managed would only help to produce more criminally minded individuals. People see the government as not caring for the citizens, and that those in government are there to serve themselves by amassing wealth. Thus, you see people breaking the pipe, carrying petroleum across the nation, people vandalising government installations that are meant for the public because they no longer have confidence in the government and everyone struggles for how to survive.

The hatred which people have for the police in the past was as a result of the fact that colonial police were oriented towards protecting the colonial interest. They were very brutal and unfriendly. In recent years, efforts have been made to effect the attitudinal change in the policemen and make them more responsive and friendly to the masses. The effects of this are currently felt or seen in our policemen. They are more polite, reliable and friendly than they were some years ago. Though more still need be done in instilling the culture of selfless service, commitment, dedication and patriotism in our policemen, it is true we have some bad eggs in the police but that is a reflection of the society. If the society is generally corrupt, it would show in all and sundry. People talk of the police at all times, perhaps, because there activities affect the people directly. In a real sense, the Nigerian Custom and the Power Holding Company staff are more corrupt. In fact, one may say that they are the most corrupt government workers. They use their offices to make money into their pockets. If these organizations (Custom and PHCN) have been manned by honest, committed and dedicated people, a lot of resources would have been coming to the nation. The staffs of PHCN behave like thin god and put heavy loads on the masses by making them pay for what they do not use.

REFERENCES

Anna, K. (2000) Globalization: Hope for the Poor? An Address to the United Nations Security Council in New York.

Asiodu, P. (1979): The Civil Service: An Insiders' View. In O. Oyediran (ed). Nigerian Government and Politics Under Military Rule. London: The Macmillan Publishers

Asoga-Allen, K. (2000): Nigerian Traditional Education and Western Education. The Effects of Western Education on Nigerian Culture: A Book of Readings on Students Unionism in Nigeria. LACOPED-Noforija-Epe: Richmark Prints.

Asoga-Allen, K. (2001): Citizenship Education for Tertiary Institutions. Noforija-Epe: Richmark Prints.

Asoga-Allen, K. (2002): The Teaching Profession: A Pragmatic Approach. Ijebu-Ode: Fembol Integra Publications.

Asoga-Allen, K. (2003): General Studies in Education: Political Economy: Science and Society: Ijebu-Ode: Lucky Odoni Nigerian Enterprises.

Asoga-Allen, K. (2004): The Role of Citizenship Education in conflict Prevention and Resolution for a Stabilized Democracy. JORELGS, VOL 1, No. 1.

Awake (2002): Globalization: Curse or Cure. Journal of Awake. May 22. Pp 1 - 14.

Bernard, J. (1957): Parties and Issues in Conflict. Journal of conflict Resolution, I: 111 - 121.

Central Bank of Nigeria (2000): Foreign Private Investment in Nigeria (1998). Economic and Financial Review, 38. No. 579.

Coleman, J. S. (1965) (ed): Education and Political Development. Princeton: N/J Princeton.

Dani, R. (1999): His Globalization Gone Too Far. Washington D. C.: Institute for International Economics.

David, V. (1997): Barrier Benefits? Regulation, Transatlantic Trade. Washington D. C.: Brookings Institute Press.

Doguwa, S. I. and Englana, E. (2002): Measuring the Economic Impact of the Federal Government Budget: 1995 - 2000. Economic and Financial Review. 38 No. 3 - pp 1 - 33

Ekemode, K. O.; Arabambi, O. A. and Sanbe, M. T. (2000): Agriculture and the Nigerian Economy, in Ekemode, K. O. (ed) Introduction to Agriculture for Sustainable Development; Lagos: National Association of Agricultural Educators (NAAGRED).

Ezegbe, M. O. (1988): Foundation of Social Studies: Umuahia, Danton Publishers.

Federal Republic of Nigeria (1999): Constitution of Federal Republic of Nigeria. Lagos: Federal Government Press.

Federal Republic of Nigeria (2006): The Population Census; Federal Government Press, Abuja

Jeggrey, S. (2005) The End of Poverty. New York: The Penguin Press.

Idowu, E. B. (1962) Olodumare: God in Yoruba Belief. London: Longmann Group Ltd.

Ilori, J. A. (1990) Religion and Politics in Nigeria. Paper presented at the 15th Annual Conference of Nigeria Association for the Study of Religion held at the University of Ilorin.

Niemeyer, J. H. (1957): Education for Citizenship, in Henry, B. (ed) Social Studies in Elementary Schools: The Fifth-Sixth Year Book of Education on Part II. Chicago: University of Chicago Press.

Nwanyanwu, O. J. (1997): Managing Ethnic Conflict and Violence in Nigeria Through Citizenship Education in Nwanyanwu, O. J. et al (eds) Education for Socio-Economic and Political Development in Nigeria.

Abeokuta: Visual Resources.

Olayiwola, E. O. (1999) Christian Religion and Development in Nigeria in the 21st Century and Problems of Development in Nigeria in the 21st Century. Journal of School of Arts and Social Sciences. FCE, Abeokuta.

Onibonoje, O. O. Civics for the Nigerians, Ibadan: Onibonoje Press.

Opajobi, E. B. (1999) Religion and Social Integration in Nigeria: An Historical Perspective, in Issues and Problems of Development in Nigeria in the 21st Century. School of Arts and Social Sciences. FCE, Abeokuta.

Osakwe, E. O. and Itedjere, P. O. (1993): Social Studies for Tertiary Students in Nigeria. Enugu: New Age Publishers.

Oyeneye, O. Y. (1997): Education as an Instrument of Socio-Economic and Political Development in Nwanyanwu, O. J. et al (eds) Education for Socio-Economic and Political Development in Nigeria. Abeokuta: Visual Resources.

Roger, H. D. (1988): The Dictionary of American Government and Politics; Chicago: The Dorsey Press.

Salimono, A. (1999): Globalization and Challenges: A Paper Presented at International Summit on Globalization as Problem of Development in Harana Cuba, January 18 - 22.

Sharfritz, J. M. (1988) The Dorsey Dictionary of American Government and Politics. Chicago: The Dorsey Press.

The Encyclopedia Americana (1995) U.S.A. Golia Incorporated

The Punch 24th November 2009

Thompson, J. W. (1979) "Christian Perspective on Power Politics" In P. C. Cotham (ed) Christian Social Ethics, Baker Book House, Michigan

United States Information Publication (2004): Downloaded from Internet.

Williams, D. L. (1994): The Cambridge Thesaurus of American English; New York: Cambridge University Press.

Yakubu, I. (1999): In Yusuf AbdulRaheem Globalization and Nigerian Economic Development: A paper presented at 4th Annual National Conference of SOSAN Held at University of Ibadan, 2003

Yusuf, A. (2003) Globalization and Economic Development: A paper presented at 4th Annual National Conference of the Social Studies Association of Nigeria (SOSAN) Held at the Faculty of Education, University of Ibadan, Ibadan.

Index

G

H

I

J

K